BORN *in Beirut*
A PRIESTHOOD

Rev. Charles L. Breindel

Rev. Charles L. Breindel

C L Breindel LLC
Danville, Virginia

BORN in Beirut
A PRIESTHOOD

Scripture citations are taken from: Lectionary for Mass Volume I, Copyright © 1998, 1997, 1970 Confraternity of Christian Doctrine; © 1997, 1981, 1969 International Commission on English in the Liturgy, Inc.

ISBN: 0-9767549-0-8

Library of Congress Control Number: 2005924469

Printed in the United States of America

Book Design: Lisa R. Gray

Author Contact Information:
Rev. Charles L. Breindel
154 College Avenue
Danville, Virginia 24541-2321
434- 793-2656

Dedication

To all the people in these reflections, with deep gratitude for their contribution to my spiritual development and growth in knowledge and love of God in his sacred scriptures.

Special thanks to my English teacher brother Joseph Breindel for his excellent editing. I am also grateful to Patsy Compton and Pamela Riedel, Ph.D. for their generous review of the draft. Most special thanks to Richard D. O'Hallaron, without whose guidance in preparations for publishing, this book would never have been. Finally, I am grateful to Richie Brackin whose faith in me kept me going to produce this work.

TABLE OF CONTENTS

Foreword

This book grew out of a day retreat that was conducted for the Catholic Daughters of America, in Richmond, Virginia, entitled "Treasures of the Heart, Treasures of the Home." In the retreat which I led, I wanted to show the participants that they could be teachers of the Good News to their family and friends by drawing upon the rich lived experiences. Using objects and anecdotes from their lives and homes, they could develop gospel messages. The premise was that all of creation displays the glory of God and his will. So we can all be teachers of the word, simply by taking a part of our lives, reflecting on it, and then applying a piece of scripture to share God's will in our lives and for others.

The retreat was quite successful and resulted in my being asked to do a weekend retreat for the deacons of the diocese. Building on the same ideas, but focusing now on the needs of men who would be preaching homilies and teaching the faith, I prepared the retreat, titled "Treasures of the Heart," to show how one can use lived experience to preach the homily in such a way that the focus is, not on self, but on the applicability of the scriptures to practical and daily human living.

Subsequent to that, the request for homilies began to grow so that I distribute Sunday homilies through regular mail and email to hundreds of individuals. More talks and retreats have also been held. Now I am compiling many of those homilies which, although they use stories from my life, can provide reflection for others who are engaged in teaching and preaching, as well as others whose lives give them opportunity to share God's Word.

For those interested in using their own heart's treasures, I have included in an Appendix the process of developing homilies and talks, along with two examples which can be found within the homilies of the book also.

[No fictional characters appear in the homilies, although I have relied on memory to create the stories, and recreate the characters as I have remembered them. No attempt is made to change them [except to use false names sometimes], but my memory may not be precise in its recall ability. For that reason, it is best not to treat all the details of individuals mentioned in the stories as certain and true.]

Introduction

"When are you going to write a book? Your life is so colorful."

"You make the Sunday homilies so applicable to us because you tell real stories about life."

It has been many years since I first heard these comments. I used to deny its truth, that is, about my life being so colorful. But I don't any more. When it was first said to me, I was a young professor at a medical college in Virginia, a father of four young daughters, and recently returned from my third trip to the American University of Beirut, where I witnessed an invasion, was taken a prisoner, and, unknown to those who challenged me to write a book, spiritually transformed.

My reply to the request to write a book has always been the same. "I don't have time to write a book." In the eighties, my time was filled by raising daughters as a single parent and working full time, both at the university and at home. In the early nineties, my excuse was still the same, but now I added the international travels that my career required, as well as the periodic foster child or stray that came to live with us over the years. [In all, there were probably about 15 such people.] When the children were grown and I entered seminary to become a Catholic priest, my excuse was seminary studies. Then, after ordination, I rephrased my excuse for not writing a book about my unusual life. I was too busy writing Sunday homilies, daily homilies, and other reflections on sacred scripture to write anything else. However, requests to lead retreats and subsequent requests for homilies reflecting the retreats' focus on preaching and teaching by use of lived experiences created a demand for something in writing. To respond, and maybe to appease, I started to circulate my Sunday homilies by e-mail and by regular mail. With this growing demand getting hard to manage, a solution came to me. This book is that solution, a compilation of scriptural reflections, based on personal stories and experiences.

Because my style of preaching is to share personal stories which exemplify the scripture, or which help to translate scripture into practical applications, many of my Sunday homilies reflect bits and pieces of my "colorful" life. It is my firm belief that any life, not just a colorful one, can give witness to the good news of Christ. In using my own life to teach and preach, I often encourage others to do the same.   My homily for the Feast of the Epiphany makes that point. It follows below, after a brief explanation of the organization of this book.

The book is organized around a series of Sunday and feastday homilies. The homilies are grouped to give a chronological ordering, using my life as the basis of the sequencing. [See table of contents.]

The titles of each reflection and homily are my own; they are followed by the proper citation from the Lectionary of readings for use in Roman Catholic, Lutheran and Episcopal churches. For instance, the first one to come is titled by me "Searching and Finding Jesus" and it was written for the readings for the Feast of the Epiphany. The next one in the Introduction is called by me "I Want To See." It was written for the readings for the Fourth Sunday of Lent, cycle A.

Searching and Finding Jesus

The Epiphany of the Lord: Isaiah 60:1-6, Matthew 2:1-12

Those who come to hear me preach each Sunday know that I like to tell personal stories as part of my homilies. I don't always do it, but often, after reflecting on the Sunday scriptures, I am drawn to recall something that happened to me, to a member of my family, or to a friend. In recalling the event or incident, it becomes clear to me in retrospect how I experienced the good news of Jesus Christ in or through what happened to me or someone I know.

I sometimes wonder if people find my stories boring or interesting, and whether they are helpful for them in understanding and living the teachings of Jesus. Since I continue to use personal stories, you must know that I think it is an effective way to preach and teach. For me the definition of a good homily is one which people are still talking about, or at least thinking about, after the Mass is over. My measure of successful preaching is found when people come up to me in the week after I have preached, and they recall something I said in the homily. My experience is that they remember the personal stories and, by then, they are recalling personal stories of their own which similarly recount some aspect of Jesus' teachings.

It seems to me that every aspect of our lives can point to Jesus and his teachings. We just have to look into the moments of our lives to find the message of Jesus. All around us, even in the most mundane things of life, there is opportunity to experience Jesus and his message.

Consider the magi in our gospel story today, on this feast of the Epiphany of the Lord. These men were able to read the skies, and to know that there was a star pointing them to Jesus. They were not even Jewish believers. But still, they were given a sign to help them to know Jesus. Then they were given the courage to follow that star. Finally, they were given the gift of discovering Jesus in their midst.

These magi are only a bit different from us in their abilities to read the signs, to be courageous, and to receive the gift of Jesus. Like them everyone of us can seek in the signs about us, in the events of our lives the reality of Jesus and his teachings. It need not be something as dramatic as a star moving toward Bethlehem for us to seek and find Jesus. It could be something much simpler and seemingly ordinary.

Consider some of these stories which I have shared with you in the past year.

- While walking or running for my daily exercise, I pick up coins that I find along my route. In doing so, I recall that these coins are, like everything else I have and am, free gifts of love from a God who is love.

- My father's recent diagnosis of cancer brought deep and happy memories of him and our mutual love and respect. It reminded me of the importance of sharing love with others daily, and not just when significant events bring our love to the forefront of our minds.

- My daughter Tressa's serious illness last fall was cause for me to reflect on the wonderful gift which Jesus' own death and resurrection made possible for all who believe in him.

- My foster son's death taught me a new meaning of forgiveness of others.

- Mom sent me her brother Jack's purple heart from when he was killed in World War II. As I reflected on his youthful death from war, I was struck by Jesus' own terrible death, but the wondrous eternal life which it brought, even to Uncle Jack. It brought cause for earthly sadness, but heavenly and eternal joy.

- When I asked a first grader what heaven was like, he told me that all the dinosaurs are in heaven. And he proved it to me with his observations that God loves everything he made, that there are no dinosaurs on earth anymore, and so they must be in heaven. No wonder, I realized, that Jesus said that unless we become like little children, we cannot enter the kingdom of heaven.

- Reading the story of how Jesus reached out and touched lepers and, in so doing, he healed them, I was drawn to reflect on the many people about me who are treated as modern-day lepers. I recalled in particular a little girl named Dorothy from my grade school who typified these leper-types. She was shunned and made fun of, and eventually came to believe in her inferiority. She needed a modern day Jesus to reach out and touch her as a modern-day leper, and I could have been that person to reach out.

- Seeing the many fences around farm fields, I was drawn to reflect on Jesus as the Good Shepherd who seeks to bring every person into his flock. When any get lost, the Good Shepherd goes after them to bring them back into the fold. Unlike Jesus, I reflected on how many people do the opposite; build fences to keep others out of their lives.

Perhaps that is enough. You get the point, I am sure. If we take the time to do so, we can experience Jesus in all the events and experiences of our lives. Just like the magi who found Jesus by following a star, our loving God gives us many signs of his love and presence. The magi would not have found Jesus if they had not stopped to reflect, to watch, and to try to understand. The magi would not have found Jesus if they did not take time to watch and seek.

If we want to experience Jesus in our lives, all we have to do is take time to reflect on the moments of our lives, the people around us, and then open our hearts. It is not difficult, but it takes some practice.

As we begin this new calendar year, may we renew our commitment to seek and find Christ, in and through the events of our daily lives. A blessed and Christ-filled New Year to you.

SPIRITUAL AWAKENING IN BEIRUT

Shortly before my review for promotion to full professor of health administration, the chairman of Promotion and Tenure review asked me to meet with him informally. When I got there, he said he had some difficulty with my promotion, and for the specific reason that he could not see the "focus" or specialty that gave me the depth that he felt should be there. Although I had dozens of published articles, had brought in millions of dollars of grants and contracts to the university, and was a competent and respected educator, it just did not seem to add up, he thought. So he began to review my career as a means of demonstrating the diversity of my professional work, and to contrast it with the lack of focus and depth. As he rattled off some of my career endeavors, he made quite clear to me the focus and direction of my life's work. That conversation changed the direction of my life, and he did not know it. I have often wished I could tell him what a wonderful thing he did in that meeting.

His comments to me went something like this. "You started out in doing rural health development, and wrote on technical planning methods. That was great - good research and publications, and service to humanity too! Then you got involved in cancer care and spent much time in getting hospice care developed in this country, with insurance reimbursement. Again, good publications and service to others too. Next, you got into church-sponsored health and human services. Some publications. Little research. But you did create job opportunities for our graduates, and that's good. At the same time, you started to work with and write about substance abuse care and its treatment. One good publication, some community service, and some teaching cases, but no depth of focus. Let's see, then there is work with adolescent psychiatric diseases, and youth suicide. Then you seem to get almost full-time involved in non-developed and developing countries, with few publications, and limited research potential. That's not very academic, even though it brought hundreds of thousands of dollars to the university. And, if we look at your related activities while here at the university, how do you justify spending your time on such things as campus ministry, and community and church boards?"

"Enough," I replied. "Perhaps you don't see the academic disciplinary focus in my career here. But I have not sought depth in a disciplinary focus, but in the area of improving the human condition, by using my knowledge and experience for others. And I think I have done it well, making my students aware of how to serve, increasing their knowledge of the world and its needs, and giving them technical skills and professional contacts to improve themselves and the world about them."

He concurred that I had indeed done that. And that I had made a good name for myself, the Department, and the University, in so doing. And he expected my promotion to full professor to go through (which it did).

But the conversation opened my eyes to see the journey I was on and the direction to which the path was leading me. And I had to face the hard reality that I had been trying to ignore for so long.

God wanted me to work full time for him, and he was preparing me for that eventuality all my life, by leading me into areas of service, intellectual discovery, and practical experience in speaking, leading, and serving that would prepare me for the role of a minister. So I began to make my plans, developing a two-year plan to complete that part of my life, and begin (Was it really a beginning?) the next phase of my growth in life - four years of seminary and then ordination as a Roman Catholic priest.

Just when did the journey toward priesthood begin? I don't think there was a particular moment, but there were benchmarks that moved the unconscious or semi-conscious goal to the fore. The first one I can recall occurred on a Sunday afternoon on a hot June day in Beirut, Lebanon, in 1982.

Read on.

I Want To See.

4th Sunday of Lent, A: Ephesians 5:8-14, John 9:1-41

Let's face it: The man-born-blind could not have received his sight any other way, except through the generous love of Jesus Christ. What is more, the blind man didn't ask for it. He didn't even know to ask, because he didn't recognize who Jesus was, at least not when it happened.

Nor did the blind man ask for the gift of his blindness either. Does that surprise you that I call blindness from birth a "gift"? It was. First, it was a gift to the man so that he might come to experience God's saving power through Jesus' miraculous cure. And it gave him the ability to know Jesus as the Messiah. Second, it was a gift for all the world, a means through which Jesus might manifest his glory and so bring many others to knowledge of his work in bringing salvation to all the world. So, while it may seem hard to admit, the man's blindness was a wonderful gift from God. So too are many of the gifts we receive in life, which we may tend to think of as pain, suffering, or casualty. Let me give you another example.

Early one Sunday morning in Beirut in 1982, a massive invasion of the country was mounted. It rained down shrapnel all day, and bullets from automatic rifles bounced off the trees, stone walls, and houses. I was hiding in Marquand House on the side of the hill at the American University, waiting for some unknown terrorists to come and get me. I had taken out my Bible, the first one I ever had, and started to read the First Letter of John. Suddenly, the front doors crashed open, and someone came running down the center hall toward the room where I sat waiting. I was frozen in terror and couldn't move, even when the blind man Jarius Khoury stumbled into me and fell over weeping.

After some moments of recollecting myself, I realized I was in the presence of a man, even more scared than I. Imagine being blind and trapped in a city at war! He had no idea if he was running from or into danger. In his panic he grabbed me and insisted we find the inner stone stairway, and hide under it for safety. So, quite suddenly, I was crouched in this small space under the back staircase with a shivering and weeping blind man. I was not aware that I was still holding onto my Bible, marked open to the First Letter of John.

After some brief introductions, he told me he was a translator of books for blind people of the Middle East, from Arabic, English, and French into Braille. He had been doing this for several years and had an office at the University. In turn, I told him I was a visiting professor at the medical school, and that I was scared and trying to read my newly acquired Bible. It was giving me comfort, I told him. That made Jarius angry. Really angry. He hated God, he told me. He was blind, shot between the eyes and left for dead, but instead became a teenager during an earlier war. They had also killed his father and tried to kill him. He could not forgive those men, nor God for his blindness and the misery he felt it brought him.

That is when it happened! I was so scared and didn't know what to do or say. So I prayed to God the prayer that has become my daily prayer. "Lord, I can not do anything. I do not know what to say or do. Please, Lord, here is my voice and my hands and my heart. Use them to help Jarius." And, to my amazement, God said Yes, took over, and talked to Jarius. God told Jarius through my voice and heart how much he loved Jarius. He told Jarius that his blindness was a gift, not specifically for Jarius, but for all the blind people in the Middle East. With his gift of blindness, Jarius could, and did, change the lives of hundreds of blind people, trapped by their blindness in ignorance and darkness. But, because of Jarius' talent for languages and his blindness, God had chosen Jarius to bring knowledge and hope to so many with his Braille translations.

By the time we crawled out from under that staircase, Jarius was weeping tears of joy for God's love, and in thanksgiving for the gift of his blindness which allowed him to be a servant of God's kingdom. Jarius forgave himself and his fathers' killers and those who blinded them. Jarius fell in love with God that day.

That was the day that Jarius learned that his blindness was the very means by which he would come to know and love God. He could now thank God for being so gifted, for himself, for others, and for God. Jarius' blindness was a gift from God, a gift through which God could manifest love to this man who had forgotten what love and living were about. And, just like the man-born-blind in our gospel story today, Jarius did not even know that Jesus was so near to him, and so eager to give him back his spiritual sight.

I guess I was even more amazed than was Jarius. Just like a blind man myself, I did not see that God was right there, eager to help, dying to use someone's hands, mind and voice, in order to bring Jarius back into the light of Christ. I certainly did not know that God would hear my prayer and use me as his instrument of light in a deep darkness.

It was the first time I ever let God use me to help someone else. I can never forget how happy God was to have someone offer himself in service to Jarius. I did not know that I could be an instrument of helping others move from darkness into Christ's light.

Today's gospel is not only a call for all of us to shed our spiritual blindness and walk in God's light; it is also a call for each one who has received the light of Christ in Baptism to imitate Jesus in giving sight to the blind, the spiritually blind, those in darkness about the Good News of Jesus Christ. Jesus did not give this great gift of sight, as a one-time event which only he could do. Jesus performed this wonderful miracle, not just for this one man, but Jesus has done it for all who have been baptized into Christ's light. And, his action is one which we are all to imitate - through our words and actions in this world. We are also to evangelize, and so to give sight to those in darkness.

Soon our thoughts will be drawn to the season of Lent. Maybe this is the time for each of us in our own pilgrimage to realize that we can assist one another in making the journey to God. Let us spend some time in reflection and preparation to make Lent what it is intended to be: a new spring, a return to forgiveness, and assistance offered to others in our communal journey. And let us invite others to join us in our Lenten journey of repentance.

The purpose of Jesus' incarnation was precisely in order to take away our sins and lead us into the eternal light. We hear it repeatedly in our gospel readings. If we would be like Christ, we too have to lead others from sin and into light - in ourselves, and in others.

Indeed, we are Christ-like when we help others to seek forgiveness. Seeking forgiveness is not just a personal matter; it is a responsibility of the entire Christian community to help each other seek and find forgiveness. Just like the blind man who needed someone to help him to recognize Christ. Just like Jarius Khoury needed someone to help him to forgive others and come into the light of Christ! Just like someone needs your help to receive God's light and life!!!

Awakening in Beirut: The Fateful Faith-Filled Day

This narrative was written using my hand-written diary which I kept during my third and final trip to the American University of Beirut, Lebanon, between May 22 and June 16, 1982. I kept a diary as a form of a "running letter" which could be shared with my family when I returned. When references are made to the reader, I have in mind my family, a wife and four daughters. This section of the diary records the events of June 4, as written by me early on Saturday morning, June 4.

June 4, 1982, Beirut, Lebanon

I am sitting on the terrace of the beautiful 103-year old presidential home on the campus of the American University of Beirut, Lebanon. This is my temporary home for three weeks. It's mid-morning here, a cloudless 75 degree day, and I'm enjoying the sea breezes that are ever-present. Hassan [house staff] will soon bring me a pot of tea and I'll relax and pretend I'm in a Mediterranean wonderland.   And I am, except for the non-visible sounds of the warring, the ground fire, the anti-aircraft missiles with their booming thuds, and the slightly quickened pulse inside me that has not diminished since the air attack on Beirut yesterday.

What am I doing here, a visiting professor to this most beautiful campus in this war-torn land? Am I really teaching graduate students health planning and policy, inspiring young minds to build a better Lebanon? I feel like the little girl Dorothy who has landed in Oz today; can I click my heels together three times, say, "Take me back to Ashland [Virginia]," and really be home?

My tea has arrived, so let me strain a cup, twist the lemon, and I'll tell you my story.

This is my third trip to Beirut. On each occasion, I have wanted to travel south sixty kilometers along the coast to Sidon, but it is near the "war zone." On both of my previous trips, my plans to visit Sidon were cut short by fighting in or near the city so that an American could not go there safely. (Nor could most anyone else, I suspect.) I had made up my mind to go this time. One of my students agreed to take me and the arrangements were made for a Friday departure at noon. That was the plan for yesterday - an afternoon in Sidon, with the return to Beirut in the late afternoon, to be home safely before dusk when safety exists no more. I awakened early Friday in order to do all my daily regimen and prepare for work before I headed for the office and my morning of teaching. I headed first to the athletic "green field" at 5:45 a.m. for my daily 5.3 miles around and around the track. And, while running, I said my daily prayers. I had some trouble concentrating on the prayers, and keeping a correct count of the number of laps I'd run, because of a sudden fear of going to Sidon. I was scared. I felt a foreboding danger associated with the trip, but there was no justification for the feeling. By the time my run was over, I felt tense and confused; on the one hand, I wanted to go to Sidon to visit my associates, but, on the other, I felt this uncomfortable way. Was I being "told" not to go, or was I a bit neurotic? I couldn't decide. At breakfast I decided to forget it all, to simply confront the student-driver at 10:30 and when I had to, to make a snap judgment about the trip.

I decided that I had better listen to my feelings and I didn't go. The student was concerned; he knew I was fearful, although I told him a lie about another unexpected appointment which had come up.

At my class later in the morning I announced that I would, after all, keep my afternoon office hours from 2:00 to 4:00 p.m. Appointments were made for 3:00 and 3:30. I went to lunch with the student-driver; he hoped I was enjoying Lebanon and wasn't getting nervous being here. I wasn't nervous, but I knew what I could not do.

I walked on Bliss Street earlier and bought a *manaooj* for lunch. That's singular for manaeesh, I've learned.

My first appointment at three was brief and Mrs. Topjein, my secretary, came in. I could not hear her well for the sounds of an airplane. AUB is on a landing course for the international airport; when planes come over, one can not hear. The explosions began at 3:20 p.m. Then I realized that the noise was not that of a passenger jet landing at the airport. I was not afraid, just annoyed. Being here, one gets used to the sounds of guns, bangs and booms. This seemed like just some more of the regular daily dose of violence. But it wasn't.

I was going to write you a few minutes ago, but the excitement started. Jets came buzzing low over the city and the ground forces opened fire with missiles. In order to confuse the missiles, the jets let out hot air balloons from the jets. The ground missiles hit the balloons. It appears that the big silver and red balloons are some kind of metallic decoys. The sights and sounds of it are dramatic - planes buzzing low, guns firing, balloons exploding full of smoke, and silence on the ground as all traffic is stopped. We assume that some ambassador has died and that this is some form of retaliation. Boy, I'm glad I am not in Sidon; it may be quiet there, but I doubt it, if it is not quiet here.

The students congregated in the great stone arch of the building's portico to watch the attack. They sent Haytham to fetch me. "Professor, come and see the show," he called and tugged my arm. Just in case the planes made only one pass, he wanted to be sure that I saw the action.

Standing with the students, I felt anxious. Some were clearly frightened, but others seemed exhilarated by the excitement of what was to come. When I looked up into the direction of their pointing arms, I saw first the metallic hot air balloons as they floated, were hit by the anti-aircraft missiles, and exploded in a cloud of smoke.

They pointed to the planes, but I couldn't see them. The ground fire was deafening. Then it ended.

We were edgy, but it had been a good show. Sima [my student appointment] ran into the courtyard in front of us; she'd seen a bullet hit. Dear Sima, she's quite scared, and after living through all these war years too!

The next attack came about three minutes later. More of the same. "Don't worry, Professor. It's to be expected. Figure ten, maybe even twenty minutes." Interest waned, and people returned to find radios. A half-hour later and on the seventh or eighth pass, interest was high again. It had been too long. "Why don't they stop? Listen to all the ambulances coming to AUB's nearby medical center." As we assembled at the portico once again, shrapnel began to fall. A big piece of an anti-aircraft missile hit about five meters from me and slid into the culvert along the building entrance. My reaction was direct and immediate - I wanted it as a souvenir. "Wait til it cools and the attack is over." I had it in my hand in five more minutes, a piece of steel the size and shape of my little finger, clearly a lethal weapon if it should fall on a person. Everyone wanted to see it, our human and macabre curiosity. When more pieces fell, the status of my piece of shrapnel decreased.

The rain of shrapnel forced us inside the building completely, but our fascination led us to hang out the ground floor windows to watch the next attack. I jumped suddenly as the leaves on the branch outside the window (and less than three meters from my face) were shredded by falling debris. Enough is enough. The windows were closed, and everyone retired to the inner hall.

During a five-minute pause between the next two attacks, I met with my 3:30 appointment. Why not, it seemed. A quick meeting though, as we couldn't stay in my office due to the large windows. I started to wonder if we'd be stuck in this building all night. I was, however, grateful that we were in this safe part of the city. We didn't know how much damage was being done, but we were glad we were not in the areas of the Palestinians. Surely there was some real damage.

Suddenly I had to get out of there. I wasn't afraid of falling shrapnel or bullets. When the next attack ended, I took off across campus for my lovely residence at the presidential house overlooking the sea. I arrived safely, despite the student's dire predictions to the contrary. There was another brief attack, during which time I was busy showing off my shrapnel to the house staff. That was the end of it for Friday June 4; it was 4:50 p.m. The silence which came over the city was deafening and more frightening than the war sounds. Shortly the sounds of ambulances, car horns, and rifle and machine gun fire relieved us from the silence.

I hurried out of the campus gates and into the city. Many men could be seen with machine guns mostly boys, teenaged and excited. Periodic bursts of gunfire warned motorists to stay away from streets where ambulances or cars of wounded would be coming. Fear and tension filled the air. All the shops were closed and bolted with metal coverings. There was little of the normally heavy Friday afternoon traffic. I walked uptown to see the people. I was drawn to the area of the American University Hospital. Lots of people were shooting into the air to scare cars away from the main road to the hospital so that people can get through to the emergency room.

The airport was hit. I've heard various and conflicting reports from the radio stations. I am feeling great stress and tension. I thought I would cry twice and didn't or couldn't. I wanted to go to Mass and pray.

I continued up the street past the boys with their old machine guns and gleeful expressions.   On Hamra Street, I turned left and entered the Church of Saint Francis where there was an evening Mass. Over the door was carved "Pax et Bonum." It was 6:00 p.m. and time for daily Mass. Outside the church were the sounds of ambulances and guns; it was a stark contrast to the quiet church with its few older ladies murmuring in French.

No priest came. A woman there told me that the area south of the city, particularly Sidon, had been badly bombed. I sat and cried. God had spoken to me, I now knew. But I wondered why.

Being in Beirut

11th Sunday, A: Exodus 19:2-6a, Romans 5:6-11, Matthew 9:36-10:8

I used to be afraid of what people would think of me if they knew that the Lord speaks to me. Most people, I think, would assume I am crazy, or on drugs, or worse. Perhaps there would be a few who would believe me and think me a saint or some holy type. In any case, everyone would think me a freak, quite outside the normal range of people -- if I said that God talks to me. But they'd all be wrong. Because God does speak to me. And I am no longer afraid or embarrassed to say so. I want to tell you why. There are three reasons.

First is that factual data that it does happen. I do hear God speak to me, just like Moses did in the first reading, and just like the apostles did in the gospel. The facts speak for themselves.

Second, I've come to realize that it doesn't mean I am holy, or even a good person, if God speaks to me. Consider Moses to whom God spoke from a burning bush. Moses was running away from the authorities because he murdered an Egyptian fellow. Moses was no saint, yet God spoke to him. And what about St. Paul who, while he was a strong persecutor of the early Christians, was spoken to by God on the road to Damascus? God spoke to an enemy of the early Church! And just like Samuel, just like the disciples, and Andrew and Peter, just like Moses and Paul, when God spoke, all they could do was listen, follow and obey. It is not that they were good or holy, but that God needed them and, in hearing his voice and obeying it, they were to become holy. God's call is not just to the holy; God's call shows us the way to become holy. That is why he talks to people like me.

Third, and most importantly, is what we learn from today's readings. God has chosen each of us, before we could ever choose God. And God is calling out to each and every one of us. Just because God speaks to me does not make me special or unique or different from anyone else. Because God is trying to speak to every person. But not everyone hears, wants to hear, or, when hearing, believes what God is saying.

Let's consider for a minute the reality that God has already chosen each of us, and has called us - all of us - because God chooses whom He needs and wants in order to accomplish His plan. And God needs you!

First, a story. It was June 1982. I was in Beirut, Lebanon. A military invasion was underway. There were jets fighting overhead, bombs falling, shrapnel raining down, the sound of machine gun fire and bombs exploding, and thousands dead. I was in hiding, and trying to get to safety over the mountain road to Damascus. But I was trapped, then captured. Lots of people needed God's love then. To my great surprise, God spoke to me and I heard. Then he used me to carry out some of his work there. I could not imagine that God would choose, then call me, and assign me some role in His work. But he did. Just like Paul who got struck while he was trying to get to Damascus, I got struck on my way to Damascus.

When I got home from Beirut, I could not deny that God had chosen me. I could not reject that call. Impossible as it may have seemed, God had reached out to me. Perhaps God felt about me during my time in Beirut just as he felt about those in our gospel: *Jesus' heart was moved with pity for them because they were troubled and abandoned, like sheep without a shepherd.* (Matthew 9:36) Whatever happened, it was the first stage of what has led me to be standing here before you today. I am grateful that God has made known his work for me. It was certainly not what I wanted at the time, or even expected. And it caused me to become someone entirely different from what I had planned and hoped for.

I didn't get what I wanted. I got what I needed. And in accepting it, I found out that it was exactly what I really wanted. How wonderful that I had to be knocked off my horse in order to hear his call, just like St. Paul. We may think of ourselves as ordinary people, good Christians, but not special. But we are special, each of us. And our special-ness comes from God's personal call and choosing of us for participation in his plan. We are each being called, we have been called, for a special role in God's plan. God has a role for each of us. It may not be what we've planned; if we respond to his call, it may cause us to change our plans, maybe radically alter our lives. What is God calling you to do? -- take care of an elderly parent, a sick spouse, or invalid child; help deal with a death, a divorce, a family in disarray. Maybe become a priest or religious?? Maybe serve on parish council, work with the parish youth or campus ministry?? Whatever it is, I hope you'll hear the call and joyfully respond.

Perhaps you may feel like the apostles must have felt when Jesus called them. "Lord, I already have a life. I do not want another." But God's reply will be the same to you and me as it must have been to them. "Yes, I know you have a life already. But I have eternal life. Help me, serve me, by helping and serving others."

In a few minutes we will stand and say The Lord's Prayer, with the words: "Thy will be done on earth as it is in heaven." When we say those words, we are accepting God's choice of each of us to participate in His work. We're saying: "May your work on earth be done through and in me, Lord. I accept my role in unfolding your wonderful Plan."

May each of us know that we've been chosen. May we hear His call, and respond despite the changes it may require of us. I pray that we all may hear God speak to us those words he said to his chosen ones in our first reading: ... *if you hearken to my voice and keep my covenant, you shall be my special possession, dearer to me than all other people, though all the earth is mine.... (Exodus 19:5)*

Cry, Shout, Hit the Wall, And Then Get Up!

15th Sunday, A: Isaiah 55:10-11, Romans 8:18-23, Matthew 13:1-23

How many of you have ever sat around and daydreamed about what the world would be like if there was total peace and calm? I'll bet the answer to that question is that none have. Let me ask another rhetorical question: How many of you have ever sat around and daydreamed about the possibility of nuclear war and total destruction of the world? To this question, I would guess that most would have to say that they have pondered long on the possibility of such evil and destruction. Today's readings shed some light on these two questions and why you may have answered the way you did.

So let's consider the readings for today. They are messages of hopefulness, faith in the future, confidence in God's triumphant rule in the world. In the reading from Isaiah, we hear words of confident overcoming of a difficult time. The Jews are captive in Babylon, and their homeland in Judea, including their temple and city of Jerusalem, have been destroyed. Yet God speaks out through the mouth of the prophet Isaiah: *My word shall not return to me void, but shall do my will, achieving the end for which I sent it.* (Isaiah 55:11) These are words of faith in the future, and of God's triumph in the world.

Paul writes to the Romans: *I consider that the sufferings of this present time are as nothing compared with the glory to be revealed for us. For creation awaits with eager expectation the revelation of the children of God.* (Romans 8:18-19) Again - words of hope and confidence.

In our gospel parable Jesus tells those around him about the sowing of the seeds of the Good News, that how despite the fact that some who receive the message will not let it grow and blossom, still many will be fertile in bringing God's message to the world.

These words of hopefulness, while acknowledging that we live in a world with pain and suffering, speak of a world of hope, of anticipation, and of joy. I think few can believe that today, in a culture pervaded by hopelessness, pessimism and negativity. This hopelessness in the world is more deadly that the AIDS virus or any other disease known today, and it threatens to destroy our capacity to imagine and wonder. It keeps us from being able to listen attentively to the word of God, and bear its message, repeated and repeated, of hope and, therefore, of the availability of joyfulness in every moment of living.

Let me return to the two questions I asked as I began today. Why is it easier to imagine that the human race could destroy itself than it is to imagine that the human race could live in peace? Irrespective of whether either possibility could ever happen, why is it easier to consider the bad rather than the good? I would contend that it is the result of learned behavior, learned hopelessness, taught to us all our lives, nurtured by negativism in daily conversations, in the media, and in the entertainment industry (if you want to call it "entertainment." I do not!). It is part of what our Holy Father Pope John Paul refers to as the "Culture of Death," so pervasive in society. This culture of death, characterized by hopelessness, is the effort of the world to counter the good news of Jesus Christ.

In today's gospel, Jesus tells us that the Father has sown good seed everywhere. But that much of the good is hard to see since it is mixed in with thorny weeds. That makes a lot of sense. In each of us there is good that is given by God. But each of us also has the freedom to allow thorns and weeds to grow in us. It can become difficult to see the good in ourselves; it can become difficult to see the good in others. Indeed, it can become difficult to see the good in the world because of all the thorns that are growing among the good seeds that God has planted.

Some look at the world about them and see principally the thorns and weeds. They want to run from it. They find life hard and they feel that their existence is burdensome. Life is something to be endured.

Others look about and they can still see the good seeds that have begun to grow. For them, life is full of goodness. Despite the existence of suffering and sin, they embrace life and all of creation, with full anticipation of finding God's presence there.

So how about you? When you look inside yourself, do you see the good seeds planted by God or do you see the thorns growing there? When you look at others, do you see the good or the bad? When you reflect on life, is it mostly burdensome and full of thorns or is it full of goodness and opportunity?

A Prayer

Here is my heart,
Here are my hands,
Here is my voice, and
Here is my mind.
I give them to you,
Dear Lord,
To use for your work,
And I will try to stay
Out of the way.

lty, then that's what we'll find.
for it, we will find it. That is
or! So why not look for good

find it half empty; others see
and weeds in life; others see
ich God has planted.

ady the fact that in June 1982
s wartime, and there was con-
vas so scared. The five days
me than the time I was actu-
I was in real danger, and that
ger, punch the wall, and cry.
ne yelling, punching and cry-
roat, hands and eyes! Then I
d my outlook on life. When
there is difficulty in life, I can concentrate on the bad things and become depressed and despair. Or I can look for some opportunity to grow and learn. There is both good and bad in any experience. I started to look for opportunities to see the good things. I found them quickly, and got busy - helping others who were scared and hiding; taking care of my health; finding food and water for myself and others. When I was captured, I put myself into a pastoral role, and that was many years before I became a priest; I tried to support those who were not given the grace to look for the good seed growing among us. I prayed with them, even Muslims and Jews, and I saw Christ's eyes looking back at me in many. Knowing God was with me, and being able to see good seed growing, even in a bed of terrible thorns, made me stronger. As I reflected on my experiences in later years, I decided to offer my life to helping others see the good seeds growing everywhere, and not look for the inevitable thorns in life.

I pray today that God will give me success; I pray today that God will give you success in seeing the results of the good seeds planted in you too.

Michel

3rd Sunday, A: Exodus 17:3-7, John 4:5-42

Sometimes we just have to take a risk, and go forward based on faith alone. Just like the Samaritan woman at the well did when she spoke to Jesus, when she went to the village and told the others, when they came and heard Jesus and believed in Him. Sometimes we just have to take a risk, like she did. I've had to take the risk of faith too.

During my time of captivity in Beirut, I had dysentery and diarrhea as did the others. Sometimes I was so thirsty and hungry that it was hard to think clearly. From the others who were with me (and understood Arabic much better than I did), I learned that we were being held prisoners on the ground floor of an apartment building in Junieh, and that there may be people on the floors above us. I did not know if the people up there were our captors, or their families, or perhaps people trapped by the war and as hungry and thirsty as I was. I did not know if they were friendly or hostile, but I was willing to take the risk to find out. I was so thirsty and hungry.

On the second evening there, there were no soldiers in sight when a 16-year old boy named Michel stuck his head into the room where I was being held. It was a stairway door, apparently unguarded, unless perhaps this boy was one of them. He motioned to me to come. I did not know what to do, but he beckoned again. So I took the risk and put my faith in this olive-skinned stranger. If I was being taken away to be killed, I did not know. But I decided to trust. Like the Samaritan woman at the well did when she encountered Jesus.

We ascended the stairway to the third or fourth floor and entered a small apartment. There was Michel's mother Latiffe and another woman and her teenaged son, all sitting on the floor around a small table covered by greasy wrapping paper and bottles. I was scared that they were the families of the soldiers and that I was being set up. But once again, I had to decide to run, or to listen. I took the risk and listened -- like the woman did at the well. What followed was an encounter with Christ, a most amazing gift in my life.

The women were widowed, they told me; their husbands were already killed. They were trapped above us in what was supposed to be an abandoned apartment. They had little food, but the boys knew when the guards changed, and how and where to sneak out for food. So they were surviving for the time being. They had learned who we were -- the political captives from the American University of Beirut on the first floor. They had little to eat, but they wanted to share some of it with me. On the table were a block of white goat cheese, some pita bread, some very bruised fruit, and bottles of water. They said: "Eat and drink. We want to help you live." But I was scared and doubtful. It was too good to be true. Just like the Samaritan woman at the well; Jesus' words were too good to be true. Just like her, it seemed too much to believe.

Then this young boy, who had come for me, said the most amazing thing I ever heard from a teenager. He said: "I came for you. It is what Jesus would do." They were Christians, I learned. And I began to cry! He took off a cross and chain from around his neck, hung it on the back of an upholstered chair, like a makeshift altar, and asked me to pray with them. I tried to, but could only listen. When I got composed, I told them that I couldn't eat when my colleagues downstairs were so hungry and thirsty too. I wanted to go and get them.

But the two mothers were concerned. They did not have enough food and water to share with all of us. It might cause them to go hungry and thirsty. I was embarrassed and wanted only to share my portion. The boys, all smiles and confident, led me down another stairwell and back into the prisoner room on the first floor. With deft skill, we avoided the guards, and the boys brought all three of us back to the apartment. We ate and drank, and prayed together before the makeshift altar. As we ate, the life-giving food seemed to multiply itself. We left quickly, taking some additional food inside our shirts and we returned to captivity. I did not care if we were missed by the guards, or even if we were caught. We had met Jesus. He had given us life-giving food and water. He had taken care of us, and I knew he would continue to do so, no matter what.

It took a leap of faith, a risk, to believe the words of an olive-skinned young man. But it led to an encounter with Christ. Ever since that day so many years ago, I am constantly attentive to hear Jesus' Word in my environment. I do not ever want to miss a chance to experience his life-giving faith.

Like the Samaritan woman at the well, sometimes you just have to take a risk, have faith in the Word you hear, and go forward into the unknown in order to meet Christ. I pray that you hear his Word today and respond in faith.

The next time you see a stranger, perhaps someone whom you would never want to spend any time with, take a second look, listen, and be prepared for the possibility of finding Christ in the words you hear. Or better yet, the next time you encounter a stranger, perhaps you can be the Christ-presence to him or her, through your words and your deeds.

May you be constantly nourished by the Word of the Sacred Scriptures so that you may be prepared for your encounter at the well of life-giving water. May the waters of Baptism which flowed over you, now flow through you, and out to others who seek to receive that same life-giving water.

Before the Firing Squad

September 11, 2002 (Wednesday of the 23rd week, II): Luke 6:20-26

When Jesus talked to those who were suffering, hungry, poor, and weeping, he recognized their experiences of sadness and anguish. But Jesus did not dwell on the past. Jesus pointed them toward the future. Listen again to the phrases of Jesus to them: *...you will be satisfied. ...you will laugh. ...your reward will be great in heaven.* (Luke 6:21, 23)

Jesus' entire ministry was about healing, about moving forward on a journey of life, into and through pain and difficulty, with a sure and certain knowledge that God's loving plan would heal us and offer us joy and peace. Jesus is for us "the light of the world." Jesus brings light into darkness. But how do we move forward into the future to be light for the world?

One year ago today the world experienced one of the worst acts of hatred, one that was not even imaginable. How do we make sense out of such hatred? How can we grow after we recognize the power of hatred in the world? Why and how could someone hate so much as that?

Let me tell you about an experience I had twenty years ago this summer that shed light for me on the cause of hatred and the way to overcome it. Along with two friends Bob and Colin, I was captured by some terrorists in the Middle East. We were pulled from our car, and made to stand against a stone wall, with our backs to the men with machine guns. The plan appeared to kill us by firing squad. Until September 11 of last year [2001], that was the most terrifying moment of my life. After some unknown period of time, they did not shoot us so we started to run down the street. We figured that we'd rather be shot in the back running away, than standing still. But they did not shoot, and we got away. When I sat down later that day, I was amazed that those men wanted to kill us; they did not even know who we were. I prayed and reflected on how someone could hate so much. And I came to this insight: Those men did not hate ME; they did not even know my name. What they hated was something that I represented to them. I did not know what that was, and it might have been something that did not even apply to me. They had assigned some label to me, a label that stood for something they hated. It was the label that they wanted to kill, and not me.

That is the key to understanding hatred. People don't hate people; they hate labels they assign to people. The ability to hate is based largely on being able to stereotype people, by giving them a label. We have all heard of hatred: hatred of foreigners, of Mexicans, of Americans, of Catholics, of Jews, of conservatives or liberals, ... - whatever. If you want to hate someone you don't know, give them a label and hate the label.

That is what happened last year on September 11th. The people who attacked America did not hate those who died or were injured; their hatred was for something that existed in their imaginations, some label or stereotype they created. And it took them years to learn to develop that label, and to learn to hate it. That is how hatred happens.

But hatred is not natural. People have to learn to hate. That is why Jesus often used a child as an example of someone who could enter the kingdom of heaven. Children do not know how to hate, but only to love and trust. They have to be taught to hate.

So, how can we overcome the remembrance of this hatred? We who have the light of Christ in us, can let it shine out into a world of darkness and hatred. We can refuse to hate, by refusing to label people. We can recognize every person as an individual, not a label, knowing full well that God loves everyone of us. And, refusing to label people, we can then see in others the same kind of goodness that has been so apparent in our country after September 11th, as countless men and women reached out to strangers to offer love, blood, sweat, money and so much more.

The world will not be conquered by hatred; the world will not be conquered by violence. The world will be conquered by God who is love. The source of this love can only be those who have the light of Christ in them. The instruments of making a brighter future are here tonight, in this church. Just as Jesus healed while on this earth, so now we, the parts of the body of Christ, must carry on the ministry of healing.

The only way that we can counter these random acts of terrorism, the only way that we can counter these random acts of violence, is with random acts of kindness, and random acts of love. We must be as indiscriminate and aggressive in doing good, in showing kindness, as those who spread evil or violence.

That is what we have to do - let the light of Christ shine out of us to anyone we meet, in any situation where love or kindness is needed, at any time we may encounter the opportunity to show love or kindness. If you want to conquer the world through Christ, resolve this evening to be a committer of random acts of kindness. As you move through the day, wherever you are, with whoever you are, whenever, if you see the opportunity to do something kind, just do it. Like the old song says: "If everyone lit just one little candle, what a bright world this would be."

Let us affirm our faith in the principles of freedom of our country and the underlying values of the Good News of Jesus Christ that enables us to say: IN GOD, WE TRUST.

As a sign of our solidarity with those who have died, as a sign of our commitment to create a better world, infused with the light of Christ, I invite you to come forward and light a candle, and then place it in the vases of sand.

MEDITATIONS ON CHILDHOOD
AND GROWING UP

Beirut was a pivotal moment in shaping my spiritual journey. But it would not have been possible unless there were planted in me good seeds of faith in God, knowledge of God's Son Jesus, and a trust that the Spirit of God was truly present in me and in all who are baptized into faith. That is why I turn first to share some homilies which give insight into the seeds of faith of my childhood and growing up years.

I was born in St. Marys, Pennsylvania, a small town, founded in 1841 by Catholic immigrants from the Oberfaltz region of northern Bavaria. They came with their priest, their brewer, and a carpenter (my ancestor). The region of the United States that they chose was quite similar to that of their homeland, in terms of terrain, weather, and vegetation. Because of this, they could easily transplant their agriculture in the new location with little difficulty. Because there were not others there already, they could also transplant their religion, language, and culture too. The dominance of a German Catholic and agriculture environment was still strong in 1948 when I was born there.

Dad was a native of the town but left during World War II and, while serving at Camp Fannin in East Texas, met and married my mother, a red-headed Texan and a Methodist. He brought her "home" to his German and Catholic family to start a family and continue his career after the war. Her acceptance and adjustment to this environment was very difficult. Her entry into the Catholic Church helped greatly. But I am indebted for her Protestant roots for much of the basis and strength of my personal faith, as you will read in one of the following homilies.

I arrived eleven months after my older brother Joe, and three-and-a-half years before Jerry. Then there was Gene, and when Gene was nearly eleven, and I was seventeen years old, along came our sister Patty. We were all educated in the dominantly Catholic school system of the town. There were three Catholic grade schools and one small public school. All the schools, like all the churches and the hospital too, were under the auspices of the Benedictine priests and nuns who had come from Germany to St. Marys in the formative days of the town. The Benedictines who preached

to me and taught me were another strong influence in my faith development, as another homily will describe.

With that small introduction, let me offer you some homilies with stories
from these young days.

Benedictine Sisters in Elementary School

13th Sunday, C: 1 Kings 19:16b, 19-21, Luke 9:51-62

Where were you when God first chose you to serve the Kingdom? And what were you doing when God spoke to you? Do you remember? Maybe I should step back a bit and ask a more basic question: Do you know if God called you?

Our first reading today tells the simple story of the great prophet Elijah selecting his successor, after being told by God whom to choose. Elijah merely told Elisha to follow him, and Elisha did. No doubt about it; this is an example of how all of us are invited to respond to God's call in our lives.

In our gospel reading today, Jesus begins the long journey to Jerusalem. The disciples had just experienced Jesus' transfiguration in which his divinity was revealed to them - this man Jesus was shown to be the Son of God in his glory. A voice spoke of Jesus as one who would accomplish his purpose in Jerusalem. So Jesus gathered up his disciples and began that journey toward his destiny. All along the way Jesus will call others to follow him, to become disciples and join with him on the road to Jerusalem, to Calvary, to resurrection and eternal life with him.

As Jesus proceeded along, he encountered first someone who said to him: "I will follow you wherever you go." (Luke 9:57) Then Jesus met another and says to that person: "Follow me." (Luke 9:59) But the hearer wanted first to take care of personal needs. A third one is invited to follow Jesus as well but that one too wants first to take care of personal things. What could be more important than responding to Jesus' invitation to follow him?!

What is remarkable in these stories is the very simplicity of the invitations of Elijah and of Jesus to follow. Notice in the call of Elisha that the great prophet merely told Elisha to follow him, and Elisha walked at this side thereafter. Note also that Elisha received his call while he was busy working at his normal daily tasks. There was no special miracle, no mystical experience, no heavenly apparitions. His calling didn't occur while he was at prayer or meditating, but simply while working in the field, doing the normal things of daily life.

There are so many instances in the Bible of people being called to serve the Lord while going about their business of daily life:

- Moses, David, and Amos were guarding their sheep when God called them;
- Gideon was threshing wheat;
- Samuel was sleeping;
- Saul was coming in from the field with his oxen;
- Simon and Andrew were washing their nets after a night of fruitless fishing;
- Matthew was seated at his stall collecting taxes.

This calling of people during the normal events of daily life happens in the scriptures far too often not to give us pause. There is a message here. What happens to the great prophets and apostles happens to us also. Frequently, the call of God, a decisive grace, will seize us in the midst of the most mundane times of our daily lives.

Let me tell you a story. When I was a boy in St. Marys, Pennsylvania, I did not understand that God could speak to people, or that God would call any of us, and certainly not me! to serve him and to follow him. Those sorts of things happened only in the Bible, and only to saints. The Benedictine Sisters always told us in grade school: "God is everywhere." But I never understood what that meant. I had never seen God or heard God speak in my life, and I did not really ever expect to. I knew that this God was the one who made me and gave me life, and that this same God was the One who came to earth and taught by word and example what was in the scriptures. But, really, that did not amount to a reason for the sisters telling us "God is everywhere." God never spoke to me, never came to my door, never sat with me when I was happy or sad. So I did not really believe it. Then one day, when I was 34 years old, I went on a Cursillo retreat, and I met this wonderful God there, and I learned that God was with me, was loving me, was calling me and choosing me to follow in his example in the here and now. It was not that I was doing something special like praying or even looking for God. I guess it was just that I was away from all the many distractions of my life, and I let myself be open to what was always and already around me - God, loving friend waiting for me to notice him and respond in recognition. It happened while I was talking with an old friend who came with me for that weekend. Afterward, I knew that God is everywhere, just as the sisters said. I came away from that retreat weekend with only one thought: I was on fire with THE LIFE OF GOD, could not put out the flame, didn't want to, and knew I never would. It was hard to be patient as I waited to see what he wanted me to do with the recognition that he was already in my life and in the lives of all who believed in and loved him.

But I had only to listen, with faith and love and trust! Through Love, given to me through the Creator God the Father, and communicated to me in the life of Jesus Christ, and in so many individuals, God's living Spirit led, loved, and healed me as my life was remolded to single father, chief cook and bottle washer, empty-nest parent, and eventually seminarian, deacon, and priest. Sometimes I wonder how many times God was speaking to me and I did not recognize Him because he looked like a family member, a friend, or someone around me. Or because I thought God came to people only in prayer, in meditation, and only in Church.

Let's admit this much: We aren't going to see or hear God in a physical and material way in this lifetime. But God is present in this world - God who created and sustains the universe, now and unto eternity, can speak to each of us -- through our love and service to each other. Let us pray that we do not miss the opportunity to experience God's call to service, just because God comes to each of us in forms and ways we do not anticipate or expect.

With all that said, let me ask you once more: Where were you when God chose you to serve the Kingdom? And what were you doing when God spoke to you? Do you remember?

Mom Was Not Catholic and Dad Was.

22nd Sunday, B: Deuteronomy 4:1-2, 6-8, James 1:17-18, 21b-22, 27, Mark 7:1-8, 14-15, 21-23

I am glad that my mother was not raised as a Catholic. She was an old-fashioned Southern Methodist whose mother was a practical woman raised in the wild west of the Texas panhandle. Mom learned a deep respect for God, based in the experiences of everyday living. Her mother taught her to respect the goodness, that is to say, the God-ness, in other people, as well as the profound gifts of the Creator that were all around. When it came to church attendance, praying and ritual actions, Grandma and my Mom had less to say. But that was not so bad.

When Mom was raising her four sons, she became a Catholic like my father. Mom was the one who sat with me each evening and taught me my catechism questions and answers. It was Mom who knelt beside the bed with me each night and helped me learn to say my prayers. It was, therefore, to Mom I went whenever I had a question about religion and God, or anything about life in general.

Mom didn't know much theology, Mom didn't know much about all the rules and rituals of the Church because Mom had only recently become a Catholic. She didn't grow up with the "extras" that we Catholics add to our expression of religion. But Mom knew the basics of faith; Mom knew the scriptures and good news of Jesus Christ. And Mom knew them very well. Mom was a good teacher!

Growing up Catholic, I learned my basics of Christianity and Catholicism, but I did not learn much of the "extras" - the customs and traditions that are part of our ever-changing and enriching ways of expressing our faith. Mom used to say that we needed to be able to differentiate between God's teachings and rules, and human teachings and rules. What she meant was that we needed to act and think, based upon Jesus Christ and His good news, and not primarily on the outward symbols that people have developed in each age to show their conformance to the good news of Jesus Christ. Simply stated, her good old-fashioned Christianity went something like this: What is most important is how you live and act on the faith you have received. It is not enough to go through the motions of ritual, not enough to pray and go to church. The grace you receive from prayer and the sacraments is grace to be used in doing what Jesus did. Be like Jesus; if you are not sure what to do, ask yourself what Jesus would do, and try to do that. Stated negatively, worry more about breaking God's rules and expectations, and less about those made by humans.

In our first reading from Deuteronomy Moses commands that nothing be added to the Law nor subtracted from it. And in our gospel, Jesus suggests a new way to translate the letter of the Law into a vibrant way of life. *This people honors me with their lips, but their hearts are far from me; in vain do they worship me, teaching as doctrines human precepts. You disregard God's commandment but cling to human tradition."* (Mark 7:6-7) Jesus makes it quite clear: Singleness of purpose and purity of heart are the standards against which to measure ritual practices and the key to living the traditions of the ancestors.

The history of our church has shown us that such an ideal is also a full-time challenge. It is always easier to perform outward rituals than to purify our inmost being. Today we begin to read the letter of James, a series of readings wherein James reiterates the commitment to Christian behavior, more challenging than merely the cleansing of hands and vessels - care for orphans and widows, and preservation from the world's corruption.

Personally, I think James sounds quite a bit like my Mom with his practical advise on how to live the life of baptismal faith. The people of James' community were more concerned with obeying the human prescriptions than with the interior and personal spiritual effects toward which the prescriptions were directed. Jesus was more concerned with doing as he did, not just with hearing what he had to say. As James puts it: *"Be doers of the word and not hearers only, deluding yourselves."* (James 1:22)

How about us? We come here to the Liturgy weekly. We hear the Word of God and let it enter into our minds. We partake of the Body and Blood of Christ so that Christ becomes integral to our very selves. These important actions on our part are gifts to us from a loving Lord. They are sources of the grace and strength we need in order to be disciples of Christ. But they are graces that are to be used and not stored up. There are no great bank accounts for grace, with our names on them in heaven.

Jesus wants us to come to his table, to pray and to grow in grace so that we have the strength of spirit to take care of others.

Jesus said that at the end of time he would judge how well each of us has done. He said he would judge us based on how well we used the grace he gave us, the Spirit he sent us in our Baptisms, to do what he did - care for the sick, the poor, the dying, the hungry, etc. If you want to be counted among his sheep, do not worry about yourself and your salvation; do what Jesus asked you to do - take care of others, bring the good news to the world, by your words and actions.

Discipleship is about bringing his good news to others. It is about the whole world, a world to which Jesus asked us to bring the Kingdom of God. God's Spirit gave the disciples the courage and grace to do what Jesus asked them to do -- Move beyond hearing the Word to living the Word. As James said: *Be doers of the word, and not hearers only.*

Listen to my Mom; listen to James; listen to Jesus: Use the graces of the Word and Sacrament to become the person Christ created you to be.

I'm Glad I Grew Up Poor.

26th Sunday, C: Luke 16:19-31

Sometimes our possessions possess us! We live in a world that worships the creations rather than the Creator.

In the gospel we just heard, Jesus is responding to the Pharisees who have mocked him for his teachings about material goods. Jesus called them "money lovers." Then He responded with this parable in which He speaks against a common understanding of his day - that there is a relationship between one's material success and God's favor. In the gospel, our rich man is shown to be one who worshiped his material wealth and ignored the needs of others. But now he had died and is suffering torment for his complacency. And Lazarus who was so poor and ill in earthly terms is now *carried by angels to the bosom of Abraham.* (Luke 16:22)

What exactly is the sin of the rich man? Perhaps in his self-satisfaction with his earthy life, in his complacent disregard of others, he ignored God's will for himself. Perhaps it is that he valued his possessions more than God; that is, he was guilty of idolatry in which he worshiped his possessions instead of God.

Luke's gospel story is a story of rejection; the Pharisees have rejected Jesus. Just as the rich man has rejected Lazarus. The Pharisees are blind in not recognizing the message of Jesus. And the rich man is blind in not recognizing Jesus' brother in the poor man Lazarus. His wealth made him blind to the needs of others.

Whatever else we might understand from this and other writing in Luke, one thing is clear. God is on the side of the poor. That does not mean he is against the rich. No, Jesus has no quarrel with the accident of a person's birth. But the point is this: riches can blind one to the reality of the economic system in which we are living. Our possessions can form a wall around us which keeps us from seeing the opportunities to participate in God's loving ministry in the world.

Being rich is ok; being complacent is not. The rich are in a more advantaged position to hear Jesus' words about the poor and to do something about it. Just seven Sundays ago we heard Jesus' words: *Much will be required of the person entrusted with much, and still more will be demanded of the person entrusted with more.* (Luke 12:48)

It is not what we have, but what we do with what we have.

It is not what we have, but how we let what we have define ourselves, and what we can and will do as Christians.

At the time I did not like it, but I am glad I grew up poor. Having never had much of anything, I did not expect to have much of anything. And happiness and success were not measured, and not measurable, by what we had, but instead by who we were. I never learned to measure my self-worth by what I had -- material, money, reputation, friends. I am grateful to my parents for this. Not everyone who is poor is so lucky as I was.

It seems that people who grow up poor are one of two types - either they are keenly aware of their deprivation of material goods and learn to crave them as a personal goal. And as they grow, their self worth is determined by wealth. Or they develop different understandings of what is important in life, and these non-material values determine their sense of self and their goals.

When I grew up, it surprised me that I achieved material success in my career. I never expected it, and it had not been a goal in my life. I felt more like the things that came my way were gifts with which God had entrusted me as a caretaker. My finances, my material goods, even my children and foster children, were not mine. They were just things that God entrusted to me to manage for Him. That is why I raised foster kids and strays. Whenever there was empty space in our home, it seemed wrong not to put it to use for some of God's work. After all, I was just the caretaker for some of God's gifts here on earth.

I did not realize it but I guess I was learning the words of Jesus in today's reading about the role of material things in our lives: If they don't help us to experience God, to work toward our eternal life instead of our earthly life, they are a torment, as they were for the rich man in our gospel.

We all have opportunities to share from our abundance - whether it is our time, resources or other talents. But we do not always do it. Maybe we don't feel the compulsion to share, thinking erroneously that what we have is actually our own.

We are all taught that it is wrong to do something which we know to be bad; for instance, it is wrong to lie, steal, hurt others. If it is wrong to do what we know is bad, it seems logical to ask if it is also wrong to avoid doing something that we know is good.

Stated simply, are we morally impelled to do good if we see it? Are we required to share ourselves and the resources and talents we have? Or is it enough for a Christian to avoid doing things we understand to be bad?

In the recent weeks we have seen a re-awakening of the understanding of the need to share from our abundance - with our time, our money, our resources, even our blood - for the good of others. How profound can this understanding be! And how contagious too.

How much money would it take for each of us to feel comfortable? Some studies have indicated that no matter what one earns, our so-called comfort zone is just a little bit higher. Most of us seem to believe we would finally feel content if we earned a few thousand dollars more each year.

Some questions for reflection:
- Do I give myself the credit for what I have, or do I acknowledge God's gifts and love in my life?
- How does my income affect the way I think about myself? About others around me?
- Which of my gifts can I share?

If you are a barber or a hairdresser, could you not give one free service per week, perhaps in a nursing home, or to a poor neighbor?

If you can read or smile, could you not visit a nursing home? There are people in any nursing home who have no one to visit them. Your greeting and smile would make their day seem like Christmas morning.

If you have received the gift of Christian faith, perhaps you could share that with someone by being a sponsor for Rite of Christian Initiation of Adults or Confirmation.

We all have things to share; it is not just money that is needed.

One test of what we consider our priorities is to examine what we do with extra time, resources/money above what we need. Where we put our extra money and time tells us much about what is most important to us.

Today we are presented the opportunity to share our gifts with which we have been entrusted by a generous God. We are challenged to avoid a contemporary form of idolatry. We pray that we will always worship the Creator, and not the things which He has created.

The Steel Bowl of My Childhood

Sts. Peter and Paul, Mass of the Day: Acts 12, 1-11, 2 Timothy 4, 6-8. 17.18, Matthew 16, 13-19

When I was growing up, we did not have much and things like decorations, knickknacks and pictures on the wall were few in those early days of my parents' home, just after the war. But there was one thing that I can remember vividly from my pre-school days in our home. It was a small covered metal dish, beautifully and intricately decorated with engravings and dabs of deep color. How I loved to play with it. I would take off the lid and put it back on over and over, marveling at how tightly it fit. I would trace the carvings on the lid of the dish, and on the lip of the bowl, with my little fingers, and pretend that I was the one who did it so beautifully.

The lip of the bowl was carved into deep grooves with sharp points, inter-spaced with small arced curves. I would put the end of my finger into the curved arcs and wonder if my fingers would ever be so big as to fill up that rounded space. What a thing of beauty and awe that little metal bowl was for a 3- or 4-year old!

I visited my parents recently for a family reunion on Father's Day. To my great surprise, that little metal bowl with its decorated lid was sitting out in the guest bedroom. Although I had not seen it in perhaps fifty years, I went to it and took it gently in my hands, like I was handling a valuable family treasure. I touched its fine decorations, remembered the deep colors and fine etching. I placed the end of my fingers into the arced grooves of the lip and verified that I had grown up, and my fingertips filled the grooves perfectly. As I was coddling the dish, and remembering my childhood, Mom came in and said that I should take that old thing home with me.

Then she told me its history. Funny that I had never asked from where it came as a child. What she told me shocked and saddened me. Here is what she said.

When Uncle Paul was newly graduated from St. Vincent's high school seminary in 1943, he was immediately drafted into the war. He was sent into the Burma/China/India theater and into the worst of warfare. The fighting was terrible and there was much bombing and death. The poor civilian people of Burma were destitute, made even more so by the war. To support themselves, the clever and resourceful people gathered up the remains of the bombs and shells. They pounded those deadly pieces of metal into dishes, cups, and other decorative items, often making delicate and elaborate decorations and colorings on them. Uncle Paul sent my parents a piece of that deadly artwork, probably as a wedding present when Mom and Dad married in January 1945. In my childhood, that little bowl sat in our living room and was my favorite plaything.

My wonderful little metal bowl, the object of my imagination's wanderings as a child, one of the first experiences of beauty and artistry for a little boy - it was really the remains of a bomb or shell, and it likely killed people as a deadly part of a weapon. I was shocked, and I was so sad to hear the story.

Still, I took the bowl and here it is. As I reflected on the bowl, its origin, its meaning to a child, and its present condition, I was struck by the fact that what was once used for bad purposes had been transformed into an object of goodness and skill. Then I came to recognize that this little bowl is just like most of us.

In our beginnings we are all sinners, we are all in need of being shaped into something of beauty. Christ gave us the sacrament of baptism to wash away our original sinfulness. Then he gave us Himself, in the sacraments of Eucharist and Confirmation to strengthen us. In the sacraments of Reconciliation and Anointing to renew us. And we come together weekly to remember and renew that gift of being made beautiful in and through Jesus Christ.

We celebrate this weekend the feast of Saints Peter and Paul, those two early foundations of our church who, through their faith and love of Jesus, brought the Good News that he taught to the world. Now they are famous for their wondrous and awe-inspiring lives and work. But, just like this little metal bowl of my childhood, they were not always that way. Recall that Saint Peter was a simple uneducated fisherman. Recall that, even after he met Jesus, saw and heard all that Jesus did and taught, still he was the one who denied Jesus three times. Saint Peter was no saint then! Like the rest of us, it was through the life he lives that he became the beautiful saint of God whose feast we celebrate today.

And Saint Paul was no saint either in his early days. He had never met Jesus while Jesus walked the earth. Paul was a highly educated Jewish Rabbi who, when the apostles started to teach what Jesus told them to do, began to persecute the early Christians. He participated in the death of the first Christian martyr Stephen, and he sought to capture and kill other followers of Jesus. But, like Saint Peter, Jesus came to him and Jesus changed him into an instrument of the gospel. On the road to Damascus, God came to Paul and made him someone beautiful and awesome. And in his subsequent life, he brought the Good News to the world. We celebrate his life too this feast day and we recognize the wonder of God who can make even Paul into a saint.

If God can make Peter and Paul into saints, then think what he can do for each of us.

No matter who we have been, no matter what we have done, no matter our origins, we are made beautiful and an object of awe in and through Jesus Christ, just like St. Peter, just like St. Paul, just like my little metal bowl.

Fences

4th Sunday, B: John 10:11-18

In the gospel we have a most wonderful image of Jesus. Of all the images of Jesus throughout the ages, what shows his tenderness and compassion more than the Good Shepherd? Even before Jesus' time, the image was used to describe the tenderness and provident care God shows us. One of the most familiar and beloved psalms is Psalm 23 that begins, "The Lord is my shepherd." For those who heard Jesus claim this title for himself, it meant more than tenderness and compassion; there was the dramatic and startling degree of love so great that the shepherd is willing to lay down his life for his flock. Though we have become accustomed to the image, perhaps we can renew our understanding of it by looking closely at the reason Jesus gives for the shepherd's goodness.

There were two types of shepherds in Jesus' time - the one who owned and tended his sheep and the ones who were hired to take care of someone else's sheep. Jesus compares the shepherd who owns his sheep to a hired hand who tends sheep. And Jesus, the Good Shepherd, contrasts himself to the hired hand. For the hired hand, the sheep are merely a commodity, to be watched over only so they can provide wool and mutton. The hired hand worked for wages, and felt no particular affection for the sheep in his care. Unlike the hired hand who works for pay, the good shepherd's life is devoted to the sheep out of pure love. The sheep are far more than a responsibility to the Good Shepherd - who is also their owner. They are the object of the shepherd's love and concern. Thus, the shepherd's devotion to them is completely unselfish; the Good Shepherd is willing to die for the sheep rather than abandon them or loose any one of them. Jesus says in the gospel: *I am the good shepherd, and I know mine and mine know me, just as the Father knows me and I know the Father; and I will lay down my life for the sheep. (John 10:11)*

One of the most notable things about Jesus' image of himself as the Good Shepherd is what he teaches us about being a leader in the faith community. As a model for religious leadership, Jesus the Good Shepherd shows us that love can be the only motivation for ministry, for any ministry, whether in the church, the school, or the community.

Perhaps even more dramatically, Jesus also shows us that there must be no exclusiveness on the part of the leader. *I have other sheep that do not belong to this fold. These also I must lead, and they will hear my voice, and there will be one flock, one shepherd.* (John 10:16) If there are sheep outside the fold (even sheep excluded by the fold itself), the Good Shepherd must go fetch them. And they must be brought in, so that there will be one flock under one shepherd. And again, the motivation for inclusion is love - not social justice, not ethical fairness, not mere tolerance, and certainly not political correctness or impressive statistics. Only love can draw the circle that includes everyone.

Fences. That's what most people would say shepherding is all about - putting up fences. That's the trick of managing wandering sheep or cattle. A shepherd would know all about fences, just as I learned all about fences as a boy. I grew up in farm country, and we spent our summers in East Texas on the farm. I know that raising animals is about putting up fences.

If you want to keep one of your own sheep from wandering, put up a fence. Then, if you see a sheep wandering about or lost, you do not have to worry if you have a strong fence up. The lost or wandering one is not yours. It is someone else's problem so you can forget it.

Putting up fences to protect our own has its opposite effect too. Putting up a fence defines what is our own responsibility, on the one hand. On the other hand, it defines those for whom we're not responsible.

In John's gospel, the shepherd worries about all the flock, and not just a certain few. This is a gospel addressed to a community that has put up fences which determine who is inside and who is outside. In such a community the only way for someone to wander or stray is if he is outside everyone's fences, if he is not anyone's responsibility. Fences hold some sheep together; they also shut others out.

Jesus has no interest in a Christian putting up fences. But we all do it. That's why a sheep can wander away with no one to notice or care. That is why even our brothers in this house could go astray with little notice. How about you? What are your fences? How do you limit those for whom you are responsible by building fences to include some, but exclude others? There are lots of fences we build - what we wear, our race or nationality, our forms of piety, where we live, our social groupings - O yes, it is easy to see others wandering and ignore them, so long as they're outside our fence, so long as they don't share our ideology, piety, live in our neighborhood, or belong to our social circle. "It is not my problem," we can say. "They are not one of mine!"

Jesus didn't build fences to limit those who were his responsibility. Jesus sought out all so that there may be *one flock, one shepherd*. If we would follow the Good Shepherd, we must share in this work of seeking out all the sheep and bring them into the one fold of Christ. May we emulate his example and take the risk to step outside of our self-made fences or, better yet, take them down, so that we might be able to see and seek any one who strays or wanders away.

My Little Brother Jerry Ran Away.

Holy Family, C: 1 John 3:1-2, 21-24, Luke 2:41-52

What is so wonderful is that they went looking for Jesus until they found him. Not everyone can do that.

I will never forget that day. I was seven years old, my little brother Jerry was four, and the new baby Gene was nearly one. Mom was busy with the baby. Since it was summertime, we three older boys went outside to play after lunch. There was plenty to do. Usually we went out into the field behind the house or the woods beside it, to play hide-and-seek, or to dam up the creek in the woods and float hand-made boats of tree bark on the water. No one worried about anyone or anything. We were country people, in quiet rural Pennsylvania, and, at least from my child-like mind, all was good and safe in the world. Like our second reading from 1 John says: *We are children of God now.* (1 John 3:2)

I recalled that day long ago as I read our gospel story today. It is such a familiar story in one way, but, in another, it is hard to relate to it unless you have experienced such a loss or tragedy in your life. There they were, the Holy Family - Mary, the quiet virginal mother who said "yes" to the message of an angel so many years ago and now, as the years passed, trying to take a family through the day-to-day ritual and roles of motherhood and religious observance; Joseph, her husband of sorts, and her protector and friend, caring for her and her baby as if he were his own, and, like her, moving his family through the annual cycle of religious observations and mundane tasks of working and supporting a household as a carpenter; and Jesus, the rather normal 12-year-old boy, born so mysteriously, after angelic announcements and miraculous happenings. On this day they were in the annual caravan of religious travelers headed back from Jerusalem after the Passover feast. It would have been, by now, a rather routine annual event, much like people of today celebrate a religious holiday like Christmas or Easter.

So, much like I felt on that day when I was playing in the field and woods behind my house, the Holy Family felt safe and calm, knowing that all was well in their routine and regular annual trip. The sudden discovery that their son Jesus was missing was, as a result, a great shock, a most amazing and an impossible event. It simply could not happen, they must have thought.

I heard my mother calling me from the house. Despite her needs to be taking care of my baby brother Gene, she was calling us home in the middle of the afternoon. It could not mean anything special. Probably she needed one of us older boys to go on an errand. When three-year-old Jerry did not come to her call, we realized that he was missing, and that he had been missing all day. I could not understand Mom's panic. Nothing like this was really possible in our world; she should not be so scared and upset. He had to be here somewhere, maybe sleeping in the field, or the basement, or playing at a neighbor's house. So we went on our search of Jerry's normal places of play, and came back to report and confirm his absence. Mom was truly scared, and she showed it. That was probably my first experience of panic too. Looking back now, it gives me some idea of how Mary and Joseph must have felt as they searched along that caravan, in a fruitless hunt for someone who was not there.

You already know how Mary and Joseph's search turned out. So too did our search for little Jerry. Here's what happened to little Jerry. He had recently gotten a nickel from Grandpa Breindel and, on his own, he decided to trek a mile into town to buy himself some candy. A mighty task for a little boy! He was found at the candy store later that afternoon, and brought back home. Like Jesus who was found in the temple, Jerry did not understand our panic and concern either. He was about his business, not bothering anyone on his candy-hunting expedition, and he did not realize the stir his absence created.

Losing someone we care about is a great tragedy, but made less tragic if the loss is temporary, as it was with my brother Jerry, and as it was with Jesus. As we listen to this story, we can feel the pain of Mary and Joseph, and, if you have had an experience like my family had with the temporary loss of little Jerry, you can appreciate even more the pain of such a loss.

So, with all that being said, let us now consider the possibility that my little brother Jerry would have been lost completely, never to be in our family again. How incredibly terrible that would have been for Mom and Dad and all us brothers! Relating this to our gospel story, consider the possible loss of Jesus in the Holy Family. What if they had not sought Jesus? What if they had not found Jesus, that they received instead the knowledge of his absence from the rest of their lives?

We who sit here listening to this gospel and my reflections are so very much like Joseph and Mary, in their seeking and finding Jesus. We too can lose him without realizing it. We too need to seek Jesus and find, or maybe re-discover, Jesus in our midst. We too hope that we will be successful in our searching. But we are different from Mary and Joseph too, in that we can lose Jesus, and then not choose to search for Jesus. Worse yet, we can choose through our actions and attitudes, to send him out of our lives, either temporarily or permanently.

If we let him out of our lives, may we always choose to search and seek for Jesus again. May we never leave Jesus behind and run away from his presence. But ...,

If we do lose him sometime in our lives, may we be able to imitate Mary and Joseph in today's gospel, and search and seek until we find him, and bring him home to our hearts again.

Dolly the Leper

3rd Sunday, C: Philippians 4:4-7, Luke 3:10-18

In today's gospel from Luke, three times John the Baptist is asked the same question: *"What should we do?"* (Luke 3:10, 12, 14) In response, John gives answers that inaugurate Jesus' teaching about justice and the proper use of possessions. John doesn't demand of his questioners that they engage in ascetical practices like fasting or prayer; he urges them to more radical behaviors related to a selfless concern for others who are disadvantaged. John the Baptizer is beginning to teach just exactly what will be Jesus' dominant message in the Gospel of Luke - concern for others is necessary for the Christian life. Later on in this gospel, Jesus tells the rich young man who asks this same question "Teacher, what must I do?" to ... *sell all you have and distribute it to the poor....* (Luke 18-22) In another place in the gospel of Luke, Peter tells the Lord: *"We have given up our possessions to follow you."* (Luke 18:28) And they did, indicating the role of true disciples of Jesus.

This question "What should we do?" is absolutely crucial. People must ask what they should do and behave accordingly. That is the basis of moral ethics. The correct use of our possessions reveals what kind of disciples we are. We must share what we have been given, material goods and personal gifts of love and charity.

To make his point even clearer, Luke identifies the kind of people who came to John the Baptizer with this question. They weren't the religious leaders and faithful Jews, but a strange collection of people on the fringes of society. For instance, the tax collectors were an unlikely lot to come to John for baptism. It wouldn't have been expected. But Luke turns upside down the prejudices of the people. These tax collectors will eagerly respond to Jesus' preaching as we will hear later on in the gospel of Luke.

Even stranger are the soldiers coming to John for baptism. These soldiers would be Jewish men in the service of the Roman leader Herod Antipas. They were a very despised lot of men because they helped to enforce Roman law and order. By telling us of these men, Luke is setting the stage for teaching us about whom we should love and with whom we should share ourselves. God loves all, even those who are despised by humanity. Later in his gospel Luke will present two other soldiers, centurions at that, who respond favorably to Jesus. And even the first Gentile convert is the centurion Cornelius.

We are constantly reminded to be like Jesus, in our words and actions. Perhaps John the Baptizer's behavior, when it is coupled with St. Paul's teaching in our second reading *Your kindness should be shown to all* (Philippians 4:5), provides the proper background for me to tell you about Dolly on this third Sunday of Advent.

Dolly first came into my life when we were in the second grade. She was being held back for a second time in that grade, and she was seated beside me in the last seat in the second row. I couldn't help but notice the dirt stains on her arms and legs, or the smell she emitted. Dolly was from the very poorest people in the Appalachian Mountains of western Pennsylvania, and her family probably didn't have indoor plumbing or running water, so baths were infrequent.

At first it started out with some of the kids complaining about her smell. But soon it became an organized system of teasing and mockery of Dolly. The kids would call out when she came near: "Watch out! She has Dolly germs. Don't let her touch you." Soon many of the other kids ran from her, taunted her, and mercilessly treated her like a leper of old. At recess time, Dolly was alone in the parking lot; at lunch time she stayed in the room to eat her bag lunch by herself. She accepted the role given to her by the other kids -- that she must indeed be some sort of a outcast or leper, to be avoided and mocked by others. Her taunting went on for years until, in junior high school, her parents took her out of that school and moved her to the other one across town. To this day, I don't know if Dolly ever got over being a leper and outcast; I always hoped that she'd met Christ and that he cured her.

Dolly was probably the poorest person I ever knew as a child. Her family had just about nothing. And then people took from Dolly the only thing she had in all the world. They took away her dignity, and condemned her to material and psychological poverty. If John the Baptizer were around, he would not stand for it. We are not to take away from others; we are to give to them - as their needs require and as our means allow. That is the answer to the question: "What should we do?"

We all have outcasts in our lives, people we shun and put out of our lives, people whom we can help but choose not to! Who are the outcasts in your life?: a former spouse from a bitter divorce; an unloving parent, maybe already deceased; a child who disappointed; a friend who betrayed? Maybe your outcasts are people of a different race, nationality, social circumstance, or religion. Maybe your outcasts are people in the Church whose spirituality and form of worship is different from yours. Whatever, let's consider those people in our lives whom we have shunned, or shut out as if they were lepers. Let us consider our outcasts and ponder what it is we can share with them in this season of giving and receiving.

Before we come to the Table of the Lord, let's forgive the lepers in our lives. Let us choose today to ask the Lord: "What should we do?" and listen in our hearts to the reply. As Saint Paul assures us today: *Then the peace of God that surpasses all understanding will guard your hearts and minds in Christ Jesus.* (Philippians 4:7)

Let us be like John the Baptizer in the gospel and reach out to the outcasts of society to share our gifts and resources with them - If we can forgive the lepers in our lives, we will surely cure the leprosy in our hearts!

Pruning Fruit Trees

5th Sunday, B: John 15:1-8

After a long winter, it is amazing how much dead wood there is in a fruit tree or vine. No matter how carefully one cares for a tree, there is still much that is useless and needs to be pruned away so that the good branches can bear much fruit.

My Uncle Paul, who was also my confirmation sponsor, taught me how to prune trees. He had lots of fruit trees in his large back yard, and he loved to prune different fruit trees and graft different varieties of fruits onto the trees. He was also a beekeeper and used the beeswax from his hives as a salve to cover the cuts and slits he made in the trees when he pruned them. I never forgot what Uncle Paul taught me. When I moved to Virginia in 1978, I bought a home with fruit trees out back. They had not produced fruit in years, I was told, because the previous owners did not take care of them. So, after some years, there was my opportunity to see if I could recall all that Uncle Paul had taught me about the pruning and care of fruit trees. I cut many of the useless branches from the trees, and carefully covered the cuts I made. When I got done, the trees looked practically naked. My friends were sure that I had killed them.

The first year the trees bore no fruit after my pruning. But every year thereafter, they were laden with so much fruit that the limbs sagged to the ground. Of course, I continued my careful pruning each year to keep the useless growth from taking over. It is important to keep the fruit-bearing parts of the plant well-connected to the trunk of the tree, and to remove all the deadwood which can not bear fruit. I also put some fertilizer around the trees too to nourish them more. Growing a fruitful tree requires both pruning and nurturing. So does growing a Christian require pruning and nurturing.

In our gospel today, Jesus describes himself as the vine and his disciples as the branches. This is a powerful image of the relationship between God and his people since, unlike a tree trunk and its limbs, the branches and vine are hardly distinguishable. It brings to mind a most intimate relationship between God and his followers. The gospel stresses the necessity of being united with Christ in all our living: *Remain in me, as I remain in you. Just as a branch cannot bear fruit on its own unless it remains on the vine, so neither can you unless you remain in me. I am the vine, you are the branches.* (John 15:4-5) There is no possibility to grow in Christ unless we remain in Christ. This means pruning away all that keeps us from fullness of life in Christ, and nurturing in ourselves that which will bear much fruit in Christ.

First, the pruning part. How do we prune away those things that keep us from unity with Christ? For many, it can be done by overcoming the bad habits that we all take on at one time or another - gossiping, hatred, non-forgiveness, laziness, for example. But for other, more difficult attitudes and behaviors, Jesus has provided us with a wonderful means to rid ourselves of our "unfruitful branches." It is the grace of the wonderful sacrament of reconciliation in which we admit our weaknesses and allow God to remove them from us through forgiveness and repentance. No one can remove all their bad habits, weaknesses, and sins without God's help. We require God's assistance and intervention through the grace of the sacrament of reconciliation. If you have anything that needs pruning from your heart, what keeps you from the sacrament?

Now, let's talk about the nurturing part of growing ourselves as branches of the vine. To be nurtured and grow good fruit, as in the gospel example of vine and branches, the branches need to be closely united to the vine, that is, to Jesus in the Body of Christ, the Church on earth. We need to be at Mass regularly and joined with the entire body of Christ to praise and thank him. We are joined to the Body of Christ, to the Vine of our gospels, when we join together as a faith community to worship and to pray. Some may say: "I don't need to go to church. I can pray alone at home." But they are wrong. We need to be joined to the vine of Christ, just as every limb of a tree, or every branch of every plant, must be interconnected through sharing in the one trunk or stem of the plant. We are nurtured in an inter-connected manner, in communion. And we nurture others in our celebration of faith and love within a community of faith.

Back to my reminiscences of my days of pruning fruit trees. When I got done pruning all the dead wood and bad limbs from my trees, there remained one task to be done. That was the burning of all the limbs which were cut off. This usually resulted in quite a large fire. Jesus reminds us in the gospel of that same effect for those who do not prune away their dead wood and nurture their branches: *Anyone who does not remain in me will be thrown out like a branch and wither; people will gather them and throw them into a fire and they will be burned.* (John 15:6)

Would it not be better to remove those things which keep us from Christ, here and now in this life, and burn them ourselves in the sacrament of reconciliation, instead of waiting to see the burning fire after we die?

Uncle Jack's Purple Heart from WW II

Easter Sunday: Acts of the Apostles 10:34a, 37-43, Colossians 3:1-4, John 20:1-9

Sometimes it seems that life is just not fair. Not fair at all. You give so much and get so little.

My mother grew up during the Depression and in the great Dust Bowl of Oklahoma and Texas. When she was graduated from high school in 1943, the war was on, and her two older brothers were gone away somewhere to serve in the Army. She did not know where; that's the way it was back then. An occasional V-mail, well edited, came from her brother Jack; he was only three years older and was her close friend as well as brother. Nothing came from the older brother Leon; he would soon be in a concentration camp somewhere in Germany.

It was not easy for her mother, my Grandma Walker, alone on a dirt farm in East Texas, and with six kids, two of them in the Army. Mom went off to Tyler to business school, working her way through as a secretary on one of the many temporary military posts set up in the Southern United States during the war.

It was in the fall of '43 when the telegram came to my grandmother. It was delivered to a lady in town. She had the only phone too and she was a good friend to Grandma. So they gave her the message, and she went down and told Grandma Walker. Jack was killed at Salerno, Italy, along with maybe a thousand or more others, while trying to land on the beaches of Salerno. There was no body to send back, but some things would be returned. Later that fall, a bag of things came - a wedding ring, some pocket trinkets, dog tags - but nothing was Jack's except for the dog tags. Life felt really hollow for Mom and the family then. Maybe two sons gone, hard times, no father, just farm work and hope.

A man came from the War Department and he gave Grandma a purple heart in a box. That was a hard thing to accept. To trade a son for a purple heart. To give a life for a piece of metal and ribbon. This box I am holding in my hand is Jack's purple heart; it's not much to look at. Just look at it. It wasn't a fair trade at all. They did not want a medal; they wanted a son and a brother back. It wasn't fair. Life was not fair at all. What good was a telegram and a purple heart?

Enough of that. Let us consider for a moment the situation of the many disciples of Jesus. They gave up everything to follow him. They left fishing nets, parents, families, and traipsed around the countryside with an itinerant preacher of love, a poorly dressed, simple son of a carpenter. But they did it because they thought they knew something special about him, and they hoped, and then they came to believe in him. They followed him for three years and then, just as they had hoped it would happen, they accompanied him triumphantly into Jerusalem - the political, military and religious capital of the country. This Jesus was really the long-awaited Messiah and he was going to reclaim the people in all his glory! Maybe it was a risk at first to follow Jesus. But now they were confident, for they really knew him and loved him. Now was the time when the big gamble on Jesus would pay-off!

But they killed Jesus. As a common criminal, they crucified him. And all the hopes were dashed. No one even had the courage to stand by him, to speak up for him, to testify to what they had hoped and then come to believe about him. Joy and hope turned to suffering and death for Jesus, and to cowardice and disappointment for the disciples.

Poor Peter. He was their leader; Jesus himself had chosen him to be the leader. Peter gave up wife and family, his fishing boat and livelihood. He gave it all. It was not fair. He traded everything for a dead man's words of love. Life wasn't fair; it wasn't fair at all. Then came Easter morning. A quick run to the tomb where they had laid Jesus. Listen again: *So Peter and the other disciple went out and came to the tomb. They both ran, but the other disciple ran faster than Peter and arrived at the tomb first; he bent down and saw the burial cloths there, but did not go in. When Simon Peter arrived after him, he went into the tomb and saw the burial cloths there, and the cloth that had covered his head, not with the burial cloths but rolled up in a separate place. Then the other disciple also went in, the one who had arrived at the tomb first, and he saw and believed. For they did not yet understand the Scripture that he had to rise from the dead.* (John 20: 3-9) What did Peter think at that moment, when he entered the tomb? More of the same, no doubt. There was no body of Jesus; even that was missing. "It's not fair. Life is not fair; they did not even leave us his body so we could see him, so we could grieve, so we could know for sure." The disciples traded their lives, and they didn't even get a body.

Just like my Grandma Walker and my Mom and their family. They traded a life and they didn't even get a body. Just this purple heart.

But then came Easter evening for the disciples gathered together in an upper room in hiding. That's when it happened. Jesus came into their midst. And Peter saw the Lord, the One whom he had denied three times. Peter and all the disciples came to understand. And then they knew that they were right about life, and about Jesus. No, life was not fair at all. But the "fairness" was not what they had thought. You see, it was not that they gave all for nothing; it was that they gave very little for Everything - for God, for Love, for Eternal Life.

No, indeed. It was not a fair trade at all for the disciples who followed Jesus. Jesus asked them for so very little compared to what he had to give them. He gave them love and life. And then he gave them Eternal Life. Through resurrection. That is why we gather to celebrate this Easter feast. We celebrate the reality that it is not a fair and equal trade:

- our lives for eternal life;
- our love for God's love;
- our patient endurance of our time on earth for our anticipated ever lasting celebration of life with a God who is Love for all eternity.

I guess, once my Grandma Walker had time to reflect on it, that she came to know too, what fairness meant to her and Mom and the family. She traded a son for a purple heart - at least that is what the earthly swap was about. But she gave a son out of her hands and into the Lord's. She gave her love in raising a young man for twenty-three years to know the meaning of God's love, service to country, and commitment to doing what is good and right. And, after she did all that which Jesus needed her to do for her son Jack, Jack gained eternal life through participation in the Easter Resurrection of Jesus Christ.

No, Grandma Walker, it wasn't a fair exchange. You got so much more than you gave; Jack waited a lifetime, albeit a short lifetime, to achieve the goal of his baptism. You got a saint in heaven, a son of yours, and now in eternal happiness. May his purple heart remind you and all of us of the greatest gift of all time: the door to Paradise has been opened to all of us through Jesus' sacrificial death and triumphal resurrection to new life.

May the God who gave us life give us all eternal life, in Jesus' name, we pray.

Dad Wanted Me to Fail.

4th Sunday, A: Zephaniah 2:3; 3:12-13, 1 Corinthians 1:26-31, Matthew 5:1-12a

When I was in high school, my father said to me one day: "Charles, I hope that some day you will experience a failure in some way." That struck me so odd that I have never forgotten it. I did not really understand what he meant, and I was hurt by the comment, and so did not ask what he meant. It was not that I was such a successful youth, but I did well in the things in which I took an interest. I tried to do my best and never to fail at things. Why, I wondered, would Dad say that he hoped I would fail at something?

Well, many years have gone by and I have come to learn the meaning of failure, disappointment, and poverty of spirit, as well as the humility and lowliness that it brings. From loss of job to loss of spouse and family, I have felt myself a failure many times, just as Dad hoped I would. Now I understand what Dad hoped for too.

He hoped that I might grow to be someone who can understand the meaning of life as something different from material riches, prestige and power. Dad wanted me to know what it means to be poor in spirit, meek, and one who mourns, so that I might be someone who would be given the kingdom of heaven, inherit the land, and be comforted. Dad wanted me to become a person of the Beatitudes, as we just heard Jesus teach on our gospel from Matthew's wonderful Sermon on the Mount. In his love for me, Dad was hoping that I might be the sort of Christian whom Jesus was calling as a disciple.

It was hard for me to understand that as a youth. It is hard for many to understand as adults. It comes as a disappointment to ambitious-minded people that God does not look for success gauged and measured by human terms. Nowhere do we hear this message more clearly than in the gospel we have just read. In poetic language we hear what a true Christian should be and what is the correct relationship of people to God. We might feel uncomfortable as we listen to Christ's perspective on what brings happiness right now in this life and not just in the future. In a startling reversal of earthly standards, Jesus puts a high value on mercy, forgiveness and gentleness. He rejects out of hand wealth, rank and freedom to do what we choose. Why? - Because they give us the false impression that we can manage our affairs without taking God into consideration. Every thing the world values as a blessing is absent from what Jesus teaches in the Beatitudes; every thing the world counts a failure Jesus proposes as a blessing. Human success and power count for nothing in God's eyes. Holiness and wealth don't fit comfortably together.

The Beatitudes give us cause for reflection as they turn our normal value system upside down, forcing us to confront whether we are guided by the gospel or by patterns set by society. Their message contradicts our common sense approach to life, yet they are the guidelines of Christ to us on how to spend this life, in order one day to enjoy eternity with him in heaven. At first sight they don't seem to be true, yet it remains a fact of experience that real genuine happiness doesn't come from wealth, power or prestige. Looking back over our lives, and recalling things which were true experiences of joy and peace, just how many of them were related to material wealth or prestige? Are not the gifts of love, sharing, life, the real sources of joy in this life?

Let me tell you a story about my experience of true joy and riches. [Point to the box I carried into the church.] See that box over there? It contains the most valuable thing that I own, and I would not trade the contents of that box for one million dollars, nor for a new home, a luxury car, or even the Hope Diamond. Do you want to see what is in it? [Go over and open the box and take out the two pieces of painted pine wood. Show them around.] These are the most precious things I own, and a deep source of the joy in my life.

Many years ago, shortly after becoming a single Dad, we had some tough financial years, with near-poverty due to medical bills, other expenses, and living in a tiny rental house, and eating Raman noodles, hot dogs, and baked beans to save money, we were on hard times. I was feeling low, and felt that my Father's hopes for my experience of failure had truly arrived. Then it was Father's Day, and I expected nothing from my kids, and didn't even plan to mention the day. But here is what happened.

My two younger daughters, aged about 8 and 6, walked into town (without my knowledge or permission, I might add), and found some pine wood scraps behind a store. They brought them home, went into the shed outback, and made me presents. These blocks of wood are those gifts. Rebecca made the larger one by nailing these two pieces of wood together. She could write and so painted the words: "DAD of the Year" on the one, and underneath: "This is awarded to Charles L. Breindel for being a great dad. From Rebecca." Then she painted two red hearts, hers and mine, on either end.

Tressa could not yet write, so Rebecca helped her with her smaller wooden blocks. Rebecca drew the word DAD in capital letters, and then little Tressa painted a face inside the letter A, putting a beard on it to look like me. Then she painted a red heart under the A, and two more on either end, just like Rebecca had done. They gave them to me for Father's Day.

I thought I was poor, and I was certainly low and humble then. My children did not know about poverty or lowliness or humility. They only knew about love. Their sense of what was important in life was based in love, and had nothing to do with the world's standards of success. No wonder Jesus is always telling us we must become like little children if we are to enter the Kingdom of Heaven.

No wonder Jesus teaches us in today's gospel to become poor in spirit, meek, merciful, and clean of heart. To such does belong the kingdom of heaven.

A conclusion: We all have riches; we all have joy to give. It may not be money, but it may be time, talents, love. You can share your time by teaching a child, by visiting a sick or homebound person, or with a simple kind word to a stranger. You can share your resources by giving clothing, canned goods, toiletries to the needy. Even a bedfast person can help others by praying for others.

You don't have to admit that all you are and have are gifts from God.

You don't have to allow yourself to be humble in the face of others.

You don't have to share yourself and your gifts with others.

You don't have to do the work of Jesus.

But if you don't, you cannot expect Jesus to say "Blessed are you ...." Not now. Not ever.

Our High School Valedictorian

13th Sunday, C: Sirach 35:12-14, 16-18, Luke 18:9-14

No one was at all surprised at my high school graduation when the valedictorian did not give the address. It was a "first" in the long history of graduation speeches at the high school. But no one would expect a shy insecure person to be able to stand up and speak publicly.

Why couldn't he speak? He was, like so many of us, afraid of the judgment of others. In reality, he was afraid of his own self-assessment, for he assessed himself based on others thought of him and he needed their approval.

Judging ourselves is a task that we do all the time. Even as I am speaking, I wonder: Do I look all right? How am I doing? What do they think of me?" It is human nature to judge oneself - in all aspects of our lives. But how we assess ourselves is dependent on what standards we use and where we get them.

Consider the Pharisee in our reading. He is implicitly judging himself. His way of judgment is to compare himself to another. In the comparison to the tax collector, he finds that he is not wanting. So he expresses his gratitude that he is, in his judgment, better than this tax collector.

The tax collector is judging himself too. But in his judgment process, he uses a different standard. Instead of looking to others to see how he is doing, he looks inside himself or, more correctly, he looks to God and finds himself very lacking.

These two ways of judging are the same ones that we all use. There is a relative sense - How am I doing relative to others around me? There is an absolute sense - How am I doing, compared to how I am capable of doing with my talents and gifts? The Pharisee used the relative sense to assess himself; but the tax collector used the absolute sense. In the end, Jesus tells us that the tax collector has chosen the better way. He has chosen to judge himself, not by others' behavior, but by his own sense of the gap between what he is called to be and what he is.

Let's examine why Jesus might have given this example and instruction. What is wrong with the Pharisee's assessment anyway? Is he not better than the tax collector in some ways? Maybe so. The fact is that the Pharisee can always find someone who has some quality against which he is somewhat better. But consider the dangers in this form or self-assessment.

First, if our basis for assessing ourselves is others, not only are we judging ourselves, we are judging others too. And we are judging others as "less than we" so that we might assess ourselves as "better than they." We put down others to build ourselves up. As the Pharisee said: *O God, I give you thanks that I am not like the rest of humanity ... or even this tax collector."* (Luke 18:11)

Second, when we judge ourselves against others, it can lead to the need to be better, not just in our own eyes, but in the eyes of others - the need to make others aware of our goodness - by public displays of our good features. As we just read: *The Pharisee took up his position and spoke this prayer to himself, ...* (Luke 18:11a)

If we start to compare ourselves to others, we become dependent on the approval of others, on the recognition by others of our goodness. Not only do we want to find ourselves better than others, we want others to recognize that we are better. The need to be better in others' eyes leads us to perform for others, and not for ourselves, or for God.

Consider again our gospel reading today about prayer. Two men are at prayer. One finds himself better and prays in gratitude; the other finds himself wanting, and prays for mercy. The point about prayer is this: Our prayer is not an optional exercise in piety, carried out to demonstrate to ourselves or to others our relationship with God. Our prayer IS our relationship with God. The way we pray reveals that relationship. The Pharisee revealed, not a relationship with God, but one with other people. The tax collector revealed his relationship with God.

Some questions for reflection emerge: When we pray, do we assess ourselves by looking at how others are doing? Or do we look at ourselves, our capacities, our gifts, our weaknesses and faults, and pray based on these?

Do we want others to see our prayer, our piety, our goodness -- in public demonstrations - so that they might judge us favorably? Or do we focus on God and our relationship with Him? When we do our personal prayer *in public*, for whom are we praying? Does God hear our prayers better if we are more public in expressing them? If not for God, for whom are our public expressions of piety?

We are challenged today to examine our processes of self-assessment, and to look in each area of our lives to see how we compare to the Pharisee and the tax collector.

We are called to recognize that it is the Lord by whom we are judged and against whose Good News we are judged. In this assessment of ourselves, we come to the humble realization that all we have and are is from His grace and love. It is He whom we seek to please, to thank, to praise.

Remember my high school valedictorian who could not speak? I am he. Sometimes I wish I had the chance to go back and give that valedictory address. I would say just what I am saying today. I would tell them that a person is never really free to be the person God had created him to be until he stops judging himself by others, and until he has granted others the right to judge him. And with this freedom, there comes a self-awareness of God's love, a gratitude to God, and a deep humility.

May we beat our breasts like the tax collector as we pray in hopeful anticipation that the Lord will see us and "we shall be exalted" and not humbled.

MEDITATIONS ON ADULTHOOD

At the time of my visits to Beirut between 1980 and 1982, I was teaching health administration in Richmond, Virginia, and raising my family in a nearby town. The decade of the seventies had been tumultuous, with births, job changes, and growing awareness of self. In this short section, I will share a couple of homilies which show how these early years affected spiritual development.

Prior to that I lived in Pennsylvania where I completed my Ph.D. at Pennsylvania State University, began a family, and lived in rural settings with children, gardening and health administration positions being my life. It was, as it is for most people in their twenties, a formative time, a time of discovery of self, with both happiness and sadness in the discoveries.

After the days in Beirut, I was a different person. I could never go back to being who I was, thinking as I did, or having the same attitudes and motivations. After returning from Beirut, I spent so much time reflecting on all that had happened to me. I was so grateful for the experiences, but I felt so guilty that it took so much tragedy and sadness for me to have the wonderful experiences that changed me spiritually.

God had spoken to me that morning on the green field of the American University of Beirut. He stopped me from going to Sidon which was to be severely bombed that day. God saved my life, I was sure. But for what reason? It haunted me for years after my return to the States. Not only had he spoken to me, God used my heart and voice when I offered them for his use. And it was such a wonderful thing to know that God would take and use me - me, of all people - for his work of spreading love and peace in the world. I wanted to experience it more.

Still, I had to return to work and family and get on with life. I had little time for musing and wondering. I had to put my reflections, or at least their implications, on a back burner while I continued to be father, husband, professor, and Catholic.

My role as husband changed in a year or so after my return. The marriage ended in divorce, and custody of the girls was shared. I do not preach on this part of my life, but use the experiences to do pastoral work for others who are experiencing family difficulties, divorce or separation.

Many other things did change though, some consciously, and others by accident or serendipity. Because of my desire for more and more experience of Christ, I got very involved in my parish, as a lector, a cantor, a choir member. I worked with the Youth Group, the Confirmation Preparation Program, the Rite of Christian Initiation of Adults, and the Education and Formation Committee. At the university, I organized and chaired a new Catholic Campus Ministry. Within the diocese I chaired a newly formed Health Care Ministry Committee. On a professional level, my interests focused on work with Catholic health and social services, or research and service to underprivileged and suffering populations - inner city and rural, mental illness, cancer care, and HIV+/AIDS, among others.

At home we started to take in stray people, mostly youths, who were temporarily without homes or family supports. Eventually I would become an official and trained foster parent. Working through Catholic Charities, there were three more teenaged youths, with physical and/or mental disabilities. All in all, I suppose there were about twenty people who lived with us over the years. I don't recall who was first or how it got started. It just seemed that we were so blessed, I was so blessed, that if we had an empty bedroom, we should not waste it. So God sent someone to fill it. The people who lived with us stayed as short as a week or two, and as long as three years. It was wonderful for my children since many of the people who came to live were from different countries and cultures. The children grew up "color-blind" and "ethnicity-blind," as a result.

As the children grew up, my work took me more and more into international development. I began to work again in the Middle East and then, when the Cold War ended in 1991, in the countries of the former Soviet Union and Eastern Europe. From these experiences, many homilies rich in exciting content were to emerge, as one will soon see.

Why I Run

2nd Sunday, B: 1 Samuel 3:3b-10, 19, 1 Corinthians 6:13c-15a, 17-20, John 1:35-42

"What are you looking for?" (John 1:38) These are the first words that Jesus speaks in the gospel of John. They are not meant to be words of an annoyed person, to someone who is following him. They are, for them and for all of us, the words which Jesus asks of all who follow him: "What are you looking for in this life?" We get clear indication of how we are to find what we are looking for in our readings today.

The theme of being called and responding to the call dominates our readings today. In the first reading, God calls Samuel three times from sleep. Literally, Samuel gets a wake up call from the Lord. Samuel responds too, with a wonderful openness in his heart. *"Speak, for your servant is listening."* (1Samuel 3:19)

In the gospel of John, we hear the call of Jesus' first disciples, and see them responding to that call. At first they call Jesus Rabbi, meaning Teacher. Then as they experience Jesus, they call him the Messiah. How wonderfully well they begin to grow in their understanding of who Jesus is; how wonderfully well they turn to him to answer for them the question which he asked of them: *"What are you looking for?"*

Therein is the key to unfolding these scriptures today. We are all on a journey, searching for something - for purpose, for meaning, for some achievement. The disciples who came to Jesus were no different; they were normal people, with normal curiosity, and normal needs in this life. They did not come to Jesus because they knew ahead of time who he was or what he offered. They came to know Jesus in the experiencing of Jesus. And in the experience of Jesus, they came to realize what they were looking for in life. And they found it; that is, they found him. Because they heard Jesus' voice, and they listened to him.

Have you ever heard Jesus speaking to you? I am sure you have. Maybe you did not know it was Jesus. Maybe you knew it was Jesus and did not want to believe it. Maybe you did not like what you heard. But Jesus does speak to all of us, and if we listen in our hearts, he will tell us what to do in order to follow him.

I guess that most of us find it too hard to accept the nearness of Jesus to us. Since his Resurrection and Ascension into heaven, we think of Jesus as far away. In fact, I think many of us prefer to think of Jesus as far away - until we are in a difficult situation and then we want Jesus to come nearer, as if he were not near and available already and always.

Let's look again at the first reading. The story of God's calling Samuel is almost magical, like a fairy tale. We can picture a young boy lying asleep in the dark, behind the sanctuary, where only one light remains glowing. He is unexpectedly awakened three times by a mysterious voice calling him by his own name Samuel. He does not suspect, even for a moment, that it is the Lord who is calling him. After all he is just a boy, and has no particular station in life or in the temple; he is merely a servant of the old priest Eli. Then Eli makes it clear to him that the voice he is hearing must be the voice of God, and he tells him how to reply with the words: *"Speak, Lord, your servant is listening."* With the simplicity of a child, Samuel obeys. He jumps out of his sleep and onto his feet in unquestioning obedience and complete willingness to serve. Then he says those words he was given: "Speak, your servant is listening."

The story of Samuel is our own story too. Samuel represents all people of no particular significance, the average people in life. We may not think of ourselves as important in life, or in the life of the Church, or in the life of Christ himself. We may feel like we are the sort of person who gets ignored all the time. But none of us is ever ignored by God. We are in God's mind eternally and under his care. He is constantly calling out to us too to enter into a relationship with him in every circumstance of life.

You don't hear him? Perhaps you are too caught up in the hustle and bustle of work, school, family, self so that you don't recognize God speaking. Maybe God's voice in your life is being drowned out and can't be heard. That is why it is important to have a quiet and peaceful place and time to develop the habit of listening for the voice of God in our hearts. God can only speak to someone who is listening.

Most of you know that I go running or jogging daily. You may think my purpose is exercise, but it is not. It is what I call my listening time, the time when I am all alone, can't be interrupted, so that I might listen to

God. That is why I always run/jog alone; the running removes the tensions from my body and mind and opens me to listening for God. It is the way I have found to make a time and place for listening. Each time I go for a run, I like to quote Samuel: *Speak, Lord, your servant is listening.* Then whatever comes into my mind as I run, I assume comes from the Lord. And I focus on it.

Everyone has to find a time and place for the Lord. We all need to include in whatever prayer regimen we have a time, not just to talk to the Lord, but time to listen. For me, it is in my exercise. For you, it may be something else. Whatever it is, I pray that you will come to know you are chosen by the Lord, and open your hearts to listen for his words. May we hear His call, and respond willingly despite the changes it may require of us. Today I pray that we might all be awakened in the night like Samuel and say: "Speak, Lord, your servant is listening."

The Boss Fired Me.

23rd Sunday, A: Ezekiel 33:7-9, Romans 13:8-10, Matthew 18:15-20

It is God's plan that all people be saved. God does not intend to lose a single one of us, not now, not ever. That is why Jesus told that wonderful parable of the one lost sheep and how the good shepherd left the other 99 sheep to search out and bring back the one which was lost.

Let me recall for you yet one more piece of scripture, this time from the book of Genesis: *Then the Lord asked Cain, "Where is your brother Abel?" He answered, "I do not know. Am I my brother's keeper?"* (Genesis 4:9) I don't have to tell you, do I? You know the answer to Cain's question to the Lord. If you were not sure if we are our brothers' and sisters' keepers, it is surely now clear from the readings we have today.

Two conclusions from our readings emerge:
- God intends that all be saved, and that all should know the way to salvation.
- Jesus showed us the way to salvation, and then he left the world, with a most amazing confidence that those who knew of the gospel would take up the task and work for the salvation of everyone, not just their own salvation.

That is easy to understand - we are our brother's and sister's keepers. We share in the responsibility to help all to overcome sin, to act with justice, and to grow in love of God and God's creatures. Easy to understand, perhaps. But difficult to do. After all, which of us wants to go and help another sinner to reform, like Jesus tells up to do: ... *go and tell him his fault between you and him alone?* (Matthew 18:15) You can imagine what people were thinking when Jesus said this: "Lord, you must be crazy. If I tell someone they are sinning, even if I do it privately and kindly, they will be angry at me. They may hit me. They will certainly scorn me. I cannot do that. So I won't do that."

But - that is what Jesus asks us to do. Jesus asks us to help our brothers and sisters to know when they are sinning.
- Not to criticize them;
- Not to judge them;

- Not to hate them; but
- To love them and to see them as a brother or sister in need.

And then:

- Seeing someone we love and in trouble, to reach out to them with kindness to help them to know God's plan for their salvation and happiness.
- To point out their errors and support them in changing.

It's not easy approaching someone. It is not any easier speaking out against social injustices before a whole group. Accepting the responsibility to speak out, to individuals or to society, as Jesus did, is only for the courageous - that is, only for people like you whose baptismal faith gives them the gifts of the Holy Spirit.

It's not easy to be a Catholic Christian in today's world - especially when it seems like few people around us share our love of God and his Son's teachings. You have to be able to stand up for what you believe. It's not easy, especially in the face of peers who think you are wrong, or crazy, or worse. I suppose most of us hope we will never be put into a situation where we have to speak out against wrong-doing. But it would be hard to live such a life, free of difficult ethical choices.

Let me tell you about one in my life. Many years ago I was the vice president of an organization. It was my first really good professional job. Finally, I had a good income, and felt like all those years of education might actually pay off. I was proud of myself, and I wanted to do a good job. One day, the purchasing agent came into my office with a stack of purchase orders in his hand. He was sweating noticeably, and he needed to talk to someone, and he chose me. He said he was "between a rock and a hard place." And what he would soon tell me would put me in the same place. My boss and his - our president - was ordering personal items through the company, he told me. He had spoken with the president about this apparent irregularity and he was told to keep his mouth shut, and just order what he wanted. He was to be quiet if he wanted to keep his job. But he could not be quiet. He could not participate in what he saw as something wrong. So he asked me what to do.

After some quick prayer, and lots of fretting, I knew what I had to do. I went to the president and asked him what were all these purchases about.

I was not judgmental, and I didn't accuse; I just wanted to understand. Well, I was given no answer, but I knew from the meeting that I had discovered dishonest activity. I went back and stopped all the purchases. I knew that I had just put my job in jeopardy. I was very scared, and no amount of prayer could comfort me. I went home in sadness. I did what I knew was the right thing. I did what Jesus asked me to do in our gospel today. But I knew there would be a high price for my action. Shortly thereafter, I was dismissed from my job.

When I look back on that event so many years ago, I have to admit that I would still do the same thing today. I have to do what my faith tells me is right, is moral, is consistent with God's love. Even though it resulted in a period of unemployment and family stress, I had to be true to myself and my God.

Tough words to hear! Tough decision to follow Jesus! The consequences of accepting Jesus' way of life will not be easy. It's amazing that anyone on the road to Jerusalem with Jesus could ever accept to follow him.

I never realized that Jesus might be speaking to me too. Not until that day so long ago in my hospital office when the purchasing agent came to see me. Jesus wants me to follow him, and I said I would, by my Baptism and Confirmation, and in my daily prayers. It was easy to follow Jesus when things were going smoothly. But it was hard to follow Jesus when the consequences of doing so were such high stakes - my job, my ego, my financial security, and maybe my career.

How about you? Have you said you would follow Jesus too? Even when the going gets tough? Has following Jesus ever caused you to do hard things?

Jesus has invited all of us to follow him down that road to Jerusalem, through death unto eternal life. And he has shown us what he needs us to do as followers. He did not say it would be easy either, as we heard in the gospel. But he told us plainly and clearly where we will end up if we follow him. If we choose not to follow him, because of fear or peer pressure or personal needs, if we follow our own self instead of Jesus, do we know where we are heading? Do we know what we are rejecting?

Following Jesus in the face of challenges and obstacles is not easy. Helping others to follow Jesus is part of the plan. It is even more difficult. But, at least we can be sure that, by following Jesus, we are on a path to eternal love and peace.

I Am a Blood Donor.

The Solemnity of the Most Sacred Heart of Jesus, B: John 19:31-37

I have a very rare type of blood. Until I left Richmond, I was able to give my blood products every 28 days. I don't know how many units I've given because I often gave more than one unit at a time. I do know that I gave blood products 120 times in my life.

My blood is a special type that is needed for extremely premature babies, the ones that don't yet have the heart and lung membranes to purify the blood in their tiny bodies. These babies have to be transfused with blood until they grow to a size where their blood cleans itself as it circulates. I'd given whole blood about sixty times when I found out that I had this very rare blood used to save the lives of premature babies.

The procedure for getting my rare blood requires that I go to a special center, and lay in a bed for about 2 hours, while a unit of blood is taken out of me, put into a centrifuge, and spun down so that the platelets and plasma can be extracted. Then the blood is shaken up and mixed again, and put back into me. The process is repeated many times until they have enough blood products for the babies. I don't mind the process at all because I know that I am saving a life each time I do it. I am honored that God gave me this special blood, that I learned of it, and that I have the ability to give it for others. Besides, giving blood makes me more like Jesus.

Jesus was a blood donor too. Listen again to our gospel: *But when they came to Jesus and saw that he was already dead, they did not break his legs, but one soldier thrust his lance into his side, and immediately blood and water flowed out.* (John 19:33-34) And his precious blood was the most special of all times, for it gives life, not just to a couple of babies, but to all the world. At the supper on the night before he died, he took a cup of wine, blessed it and gave it to his disciples, saying: *"Drink from it, all of you, for this is my blood of the covenant, which will be shed on behalf of many for the forgiveness of sins...."* (Matthew 26:27-28)

We celebrate this evening the feast of the Sacred Heart of Jesus, a feast which calls us to remember Jesus as one whose heart bled for all the world, bringing salvation through the forgiveness of sins, and an invitation to share in his work and love on earth.

Our parish is named in honor of the Sacred Heart of Jesus. In choosing that name for our parish 125 years ago, the bishop and people must have recognized the very special experience of Jesus' love in the Dan River Valley. That love grew from the moment the first Mass in Danville was celebrated in Mr. Kelley's tailor shop in 1875 by a visiting priest from Lynchburg. That priest Father J J McGurk later canvassed the community for several days and collected $800 toward the construction of a church. He returned the following year with the Bishop of Richmond (later Cardinal) Gibbons to seek out a Catholic community and the possibility of locating a parish in Danville. A Catholic aid society was formed in August 1876 to devise plans for a permanent church. With additional funds from the Bishop and from the parish community of the Richmond Cathedral, a triangular property at the junction of Ross and North Holbrook Streets was acquired for the location of the church. The first church building was completed in June 1878. That fall the bishop came and dedicated the church as the parish of Sacred Heart.

The love of Christ, poured out as blood on the cross, now was poured with love on the people of Danville. We celebrate this year the wonderful gift of Christ's love for us these 125 years, with a series of special events. They draw attention to our gratitude for our faith, our faith community and our Catholic heritage.

This is a special year for us here at Sacred Heart. May we all open our hearts to the experience of our Catholic parish, made possible by the blood of the Most Sacred Heart of Jesus, by joining in the many events that celebrate our local Catholic Church. As Jesus opened his Sacred Heart to share his love, may we open our hearts and so that we can share in the work of Jesus' kingdom here in the Dan River Valley.

John the Baptist Became My Role Model.

3rd Sunday of Advent, B: Isaiah 61:1-2a, 10-11, John 1:6-8, 19-28

When I was captured in Beirut in June 1982, I spent the first two days in shock. But as the days progressed, more people were being rounded up until there was a crowded room of panicking people being held at gunpoint. Without knowing why or how, I began to take care of the others; they seemed worse off than I was. I tried to calm those with panic attacks, found something for those who were hungry or thirsty, or just plain scared, I prayed with some, and tried to show them an ounce of love in an environment where love no longer seemed possible.

When we eventually got our freedom, I learned that many of the other captives had thought that I was an experienced Christian minister of some type. That amazed me, because, at that time, I was a visiting professor to the Medical School; I had no counseling training and little religious training. What struck me was this: They recognized me as a Christian by my actions! They somehow felt God's presence in my actions and words! The thought of that would change my life. I began to want to know more about how to be a good Christian, how to be like Christ.

John the Baptist became a model for me in how to do this. In today's gospel, we hear of this man John the Baptist who was doing what he was called to do, and hoping that those about him would see, not him, but the One to whom his life was pointing, Jesus, the Messiah-arrived-at-last, the very Son of God.

They asked John the Baptist: Who are you? And in so doing, they do not understand what he is telling them. When John replies, he points out that, instead of wondering who he is, they should be noticing another among themselves, and asking who He is. John tells them: ... *there is one among you whom you do not recognize, the one who is coming after me, ...* (John 1:26-27) John wants them to notice Jesus, not him.

Let us take the amazing words of John the Baptist and apply them to ourselves. If someone asked you, as a Catholic Christian, "Who are you?" what would you say? Would you say something about yourself or about Christ, as did John the Baptist? I think we'd all have difficulty saying who we are as followers of Christ. We can agree with John the Baptist that our lives are pointing to Christ. In this regard John the Baptist is a very good role model for any Christian - Live in such a way that one can recognize you as a follower of Christ; live so that others see Christ when they see you.

Our gospel reading stops short in telling us all that John the Baptist said about himself. A little further along in the gospel of John, John the Baptist completes his own understanding of who he was and why he lives, in his final speech of the gospel. Speaking of Jesus he says: *He must increase; I must decrease.* (John 3:30)

John's statement has two parts. First, John says that what is important about himself is to whom his life is pointing. It is pointing to someone else - Jesus. *I am the voice of one crying out in the desert, make straight the way of the Lord ...* (John 1:23), he says. His second point is that it is less important who he is, but more important who Jesus is. John does not want them to focus on him; he wants them to focus on the *one among you whom you do not recognize, the one who is coming after me, whose sandal strap I am not worthy to untie.* (John 1:26-27)

John wants to live his life so that, when people look at him, they see Christ instead. That is exactly my own goal as a Christian, a Catholic, and a priest. From that very first time it happened in Beirut so long ago, I want my life to point to Christ. When I speak, I hope that people will hear Christ's words and not mine. When I act, I hope that people will see Christ acting, and not me. Like John, I say those same words about myself: *He must increase; I must decrease.* (John 3:30)

I pray that, as I grow and mature, I may become more and more like John the Baptist. I pray that, as I take into myself the daily Eucharist and the daily scriptures, eventually I will be entirely filled up with Christ so that I become transparent, and only Christ can be seen in me. Perhaps when that happens, I'll be able to be lifted up into his arms and be with Christ forever.

Today, I pray the same for you. May each of us become like the Baptist, living a life that points to Christ with such convincing faith that we become transparent, and that Christ becomes everything in us. May we all be able to say those words from our first reading from Isaiah: *The spirit of the Lord GOD is upon me, because the LORD has anointed me; he has sent me to bring glad tidings to the poor, to heal the brokenhearted, to proclaim liberty to the captives and release to the prisoners, to announce a year of favor from the LORD and a day of vindication by our God.* (Isaiah 61:1-2)

May God bless you all, fill you with his love until you overflow and glow with a Christmas presence.

I Never Gave My Daughters an Allowance.

Feast of the Holy Family, B: Genesis 15:1-6; 21:1-3, Hebrews 11:8, 11-12, 17-19, Luke 2:22-40

It seemed strange to many of my friends too and they often told me so. But I never paid my children an allowance - not a weekly bit of cash like so many other of their friends got. Nor did they ever get paid for doing any chores around the house or lawn. The kids never complained or cared either. I'll tell you why I did not give them an allowance. It relates to how I see the meaning of the word "family."

From my experiences, it seems that a family is a group of people whose collective activities, energies, and attitudes makes a home. Each person who is a member of a family contributes to the good of the whole family, not because they are forced to do so, not because they are paid to do so, but because there is no family where there is no commitment to the whole. I also never assigned particular chores to the girls. Using the same under-standing of what makes a family, I taught them instead all the various ways in which they could share their time and energies to build up the home and "make it work" - laundry, cooking, doing the dishes, taking out the trash, dusting, sweeping, and lots more. Then I taught them that being a member of the family meant doing whatever one could do, whenever one saw something that needed done. So, if one of them would see the trash need-ed to go out, they should take it out. If they put their dirty clothes in the laundry room and they saw there was enough for a load, they should do it.

Now all this may seem strange to you. As I tell it to you, I have to admit it seems odd to me, even now. But it was what we did. It was how we made a family. And, for us, it worked. I am not advocating this for anyone else either. Everyone has to find their own way of making a house a home, and a group of people into a family.

What I learned in raising my own family is the crucial role of faith and hope and love in building a family. In having faith in each to be what we could be, in trusting that we would each do what was needed for the good of all, in expressing hope that we could and would become what God wanted us to be, and in loving each other with respect for our individual needs and differences, we made a family. I think we formed a good family. Upon reflection, I believe I was a good parent, making a family based in faith and hope and love. That is what makes a "family" holy. Today's readings affirm the meaning of family - family exists wherever and whenever a group of people live in mutual faith, hope and love.

Today is the Feast of the Holy Family. The Holy Family of which we read exemplified faith. What else could one call it that a man, based simply upon the words of an angel in a dream, would trust his life, and his new wife and her son, to a belief in God's words about a baby to be born miraculously? What else could you call it that a young virgin would say "Yes" to an angel and offer her life with complete openness to God's service? Yes, the holy family was a family of faith. The faith of the Holy Family is a model for any family of faith in each other - even as was my faith in my children, or the faith that we have in each other who are here today.

The Holy Family was also a family of hope. For, to have hope means to have expectations. One cannot hope unless there is something to hope for. Both Mary and Joseph hoped that the messages of the angel might be fulfilled, that the risk they took in saying "Yes" to something they could not fully understand, might be achieved in this son of theirs, Jesus. They kept hope, even when it seemed impossible, such as when they had to flee into Egypt or when Jesus was lost for three days. Hope too is what makes a family. And so again is the Holy Family a model for any family of hope - even as I had hopes for my girls, even as we all have hopes for each other in this Christian community.

But, most of all, it is love which grounds faith and hope. We can love those we believe in; we can love those in whom we hope. Love is the basis for family - a love that trusts when trust seems impossible, a love that keeps hope alive, even when despair is imminent. It is the love of Jesus, and of Mary and Joseph for each other - a mirror of their love for the God who created them individually and made them, through the power of the Holy Spirit, into a family, into The Holy Family - that makes them above all our model of what it means to live as a family.

Today we praise God for the gift of the Holy Family, for they show the meaning and purpose of family to all who seek to live as a family here on earth, and who work to become one family in Christ Jesus. We become family, as Jesus, Mary and Joseph show us by their lives, through the daily enactment of faith in each other, hope for each other, and love - a love that is based in working together each day to make our love a visible sign of God's love here and now.

My prayer today is that the family gathered here might also one day come to experience tears of joy - perhaps the joyful tears of Christ himself as he welcomes us home into his Eternal Triune Family.

Thirsting for Water Overseas

3rd Sunday of Lent, A: Exodus 17:3-7, Romans 5:1-2, 5-8, John 4:5-42

I don't suppose many people get the opportunity in a lifetime to experience a real lack of water, one that makes thirst so powerful that it is hard to think of anything but water. I've had that experience of having my mind saturated with craving for water. First, it was in Egypt when I was stranded south of Cairo about 270 kilometers. There was no water to drink, only the Nile, and it was so polluted that is served as the local sink, toilet, bathtub, and garbage disposal plant. In desperation I drank it boiled; as a result, I nearly died of enteric disease. A couple of years later, in Lebanon, during war time, and while being held prisoner, there was neither food or water for several days; my mind turned to water, and it was an obsession to think of my thirst. Day dreaming about water, clean and clear; it was hard to think of anything else. When that ended I vowed that I'd never be thirsty again. Just like in the movie Gone with the Wind, when Scarlett O'Hara says in her hunger: "As God is my witness, I will never be hungry again," so did I proclaim my promise never to know thirst again. But, I only half-achieved my self-promise. A decade later, I was in Eastern Siberia, in Khabarovsk, where there was no water fit to drink, and only some bottled Chinese beer and cheap street vodka available. I bought a bottle of each, and boarded the Trans-Siberian Railroad, heading for Vladivostok, about 14 hours distant. I was so scared that there would be no water to drink at the end of my journey that I parceled out in single mouthfuls the beer. And the vodka I used to brush my teeth and wash my hands. Honest!

Looking back on these most unusual experiences, I am grateful for the rare experiences of deep thirst. For as I listen to our readings today, I can relate to their reflections on being thirsty, really thirsty, so thirsty that there is room in the mind for nothing else but thoughts of thirst and quenching water. Would that my thirst for God could be so overwhelming!

In today's readings we hear much about this thirsting, this longing for water, only the thirsting for water becomes a metaphor for the thirsting for God in the world.

In our first reading, the wandering Israelites are physically thirsty; they want water. God, miraculously providing it, meets their needs. But note that this incident of the people's calling out to God to assuage their thirst is not given to us as an example of faith; on the contrary, it becomes proverbial in the Scriptures as an example of sin. The psalm exhorts us; "harden not your hearts as at Meribah, as in the day of Massah in the desert." It is an example of precisely what faith is not. The Israelites, we are told, "tested" God: that is, they did not believe in God's goodness and mystery, but insisted that God must meet their needs, on their terms. Their "thirst" is not really for God, but simply for water. From the scriptural point of view, this is hardness of heart. It symbolizes a sinful kind of religion that wishes to use God as means to some other goal - physical, emotional, or psychological - that is the real object of our desire.

By contrast, the gospel presents us with an example of real faith, a thirst for God that slowly progresses. The Samaritan woman at the well really recognizes Christ when she forgets her own material thirst for water - her initial interest - and allows a new thirst to emerge, a thirst for "living water" whose existence she has not even suspected. Her progressive insight parallels and symbolizes the process of conversion: a movement out of our world and our apparent needs, to the level of what we are really made for and thirsting for.

The story of the woman at the well is particularly suited for our Elect in the RCIA program as they prepare for baptism at Easter: it symbolizes their deepening of faith from an initial attraction, which may have many motivations, to our encounter with the living mystery of God. It is also a challenge for all Christians: do we have a religion of thirst or of satisfaction? A religion that claims to have all the answers, or one that involves us in ever deeper questions, more wonder and mystery? A religion that sees God as fulfilling our needs, or one that recognizes that God is what we desire?

There is a second important point to Jesus' encounter with the non-Jewish Samaritan woman at the well. It is our common baptism and faith which unites us all in communion. In our gospel, Jews and Samaritans are divided; they find many differences that overcome any ability to see each other as being the same. But they are the same in at least this way: They are both thirsting for God. And the perfect symbol of that thirst for God is our everyday thirst for water. Next to carbon, the thing that all life forms have most in common is water. We human beings begin our early development floating in the amniotic fluid of our mother's womb. Once out of that sea-like environment, our bodies insist that we continue to imbibe water, first in our mother's milk, then wherever we can find it, all the days of our life. The desire and need for water never ceases as a means of giving earthly life. So too should the thirst for God never cease as a means of giving eternal life.

It seems to me that there is in our modern world such a thirsting for God. We see it everywhere, but the news seems to report only the negative form of that thirst for God - the fundamentalism that leads people to associate their religious views with political, cultural, and economic interests - fanatics in Ireland, the Middle East, and the United States who, under the presumption of religion - seek to impose on others their view of God and the world. There is, however, much positive about the longing for God, the thirsting for a relationship with the divine.

If it is a true thirst, a real longing, then just as thirst for water saturates the mind, so does the thirst for God. Just as the woman at the well was surprised at where and how she would find the life-giving water, so too need we be prepared to discover just how and where we might be nourished and refreshed with the water of life as we search to satisfy our longing for God in our lives. The woman at the well met a stranger at a well. Perhaps you too will meet such a "stranger;" so look carefully at the people who come into your life. The next time you see a stranger, perhaps someone whom you would never want to spend any time with, you might pause and take a second look, then listen, and be prepared for the possibility of finding Christ in the person you meet or the words you hear. Or better yet, the next time you encounter a stranger, perhaps you can be the Christ-presence to him or her, through your words and your deeds.

May our thirst for the life-giving water of Christ overwhelm us with longing and love.

May we be constantly nourished by the Word of the Sacred Scriptures so that we may be prepared for our encounter at the well of life-giving water.

May the water of Baptism which flowed over you, now flow through you, and out to others who seek to receive that same life-giving water of Christ.

Visits to Churches in Egypt and Siberia

28th Sunday, B: Wisdom 7:7-11, Mark 10:17-30

The church I attended in rural Egypt was located about 270 kilometers south of Cairo. It was made of sandstone and mud, decorated with hand-painted stones, and not much else. The windows were holes in the wall to let in air and light. The altar, chair and stand were made of crude boards from the limited palm trees nearby. Only one light was present - a sanctuary lamp burned, filled with palm oil. The priest's vestments were meager and few. Most important of all, I seemed to be the only one who noticed all these things. I was the only one who did not seem to feel that I was in a church.

At that time I never thought I would ever see a poor church like that again. But I was wrong. For my career took me to many underdeveloped places in the world, even to places where churches were illegal. Let me tell you about one such place.

Years later, while working in the countries of the former Soviet Union, I was assigned to a project in Vladivostok, Russia, on the eastern coast of Siberia, just north of Korea, and across the sea from Japan. I tried to find a church to attend Mass. It was very difficult to find a priest, much less a church. But one did exist and, when located, I found a small Christian community gathered in the barren first-floor activity room of an old Soviet apartment building. It was strange to be in such a dingy room, with its cracked glass windowpanes, and old cheap furniture made for a Communist commune. Stranger still was the wonderful feeling of Christian community and fellowship which the prayers and the Eucharist evoked in all who gathered in that dimly lit room to celebrate Liturgy.

During the third year of my work in that region, the people decided it was time to build or recover a church building for their Sunday worship. The economic situation made it possible at last to begin to spend money on restoring the old church on the hillside which overlooked the harbor. That's when the troubles in the community started.

First, they began to argue about whether to try to restore the church or build a new one. The old one was from the days prior to 1921, when it was taken over by the Communists, gutted, and turned into a storage warehouse. Its condition was terrible, having had little or no repairs to the stone and wooden structure in at least 70 years. Now, the once-loving community was divided in half, based on this painful struggle. But, once it was decided to try to renovate this old building, another series of arguments and fighting began in the community. It seems that everyone wanted the church to look like the church they remembered from their own youth, or heard of from their parents. The problem was complicated because the people of the Vladivostok area were very diverse. Many came to the area as political prisoners during the Soviet era, or as war prisoners or refugees during the Second World War, and they represented people of both Orthodox and other Christian traditions. There were Ukranians, Albanians, Germans, Russians, Poles, and Slavs; and their customs of liturgy and church design and style were as different as can be. It was hard to find any common ground to go forward in the renovation of the church.

- Some wanted icons, others paintings, still others statues. Some found all such things as idols, and wanted none of that form of decoration.
- Some wanted chairs, some did not. Some wanted kneelers; some did not.
- Some wanted candles, others oil lamps, and others nothing but natural light.
- Some said the floor should be carpeted by layers of rugs, others said it must be stone.

And so the arguments went on.

It was hard to believe that this was the same warm community which had been meeting in a barren apartment building room, with nothing but each other to make a people into a holy and Spirit-filled church.

It was incredible that these same folks had kept their Christian faith alive, but underground, for nearly 75 years, with nothing more than their memories, their behavior, and their gatherings in secret with some scripture and traditions. Now they had money, access to resources, and suddenly, their material goods overshadowed their sense of community, of liturgy, of religious understanding.

I think, perhaps, that what Christ said to the rich young man in our gospel today, might be applied equally well to a gathered community. In today's Gospel we encounter the very sincere young man who comes to

Jesus to ask what more he might do to inherit eternal life. Jesus points to his riches, his many material possessions, and says: "You are lacking in one thing. Go, sell what you have, and give to the poor and you will have treasure in heaven; then come, follow me." The young man seemed surprised. He wanted another rule he could follow, another commandment he could obey. But what he got was an offer of eternal life, based on a freedom from the concerns and goods of this earthly life. It was clearly not what the young man expected, not what he wanted. Obviously, he saw himself as integral to what he owned. He defined himself based on his possessions. He could not give up these things for, to do so, would be to give up his understanding of who he was.

It's not just people who define themselves based on what they have, what they wear or place about themselves, and how they decorate themselves and their environments. Jesus wanted the man to grow beyond his limited understanding of who he is, based on earthly goods. Some people also define what their church is, where they can and how they should celebrate Liturgy, based on the material and earthly goods and decorations that are present. They limit their understanding of what is Christian Liturgy and the Catholic church, based on the material things present and the decorations used, and not on the reality of Christ's presence in the sacred scriptures, the Eucharist and the gathered assembly.

I see Jesus' point to that young man. It seems that the more we have, the more we spend time and energy worrying about it — what to do with what we have, what to buy, what to use, and so on. Having much, whether it be an individual person, or a church community, can be a real distraction from living Christian discipleship.

Jesus doesn't say that having riches is bad. Jesus simply points out how hard it is for folks who have riches to enter the kingdom of heaven. It is not the wealth he criticizes; it is the distractions which the wealth can bring. It is the preoccupation that wealth can create for us to focus on earthly things and not the divine. It is not possessions that matter, unless we let our possessions possess us.

It is similar with our liturgy. Being concerned about the beauty and decor of our church and our liturgy is not a problem but can be a source of love and grace, but it becomes a problem if we let our focus on such things keep us from the meaning that the building and its beauty point toward.

Sometimes I recall those primitive encounters with the mystery of Christ in the Liturgy, and I am nostalgic, even wishful, that I could experience those lovely Christian Liturgy again. It took so little to experience so much love — only some bread and wine, the scriptures, and a community of people who shared a love for each other, based on the reality of Christ's presence — in the Eucharist, in the scripture, in the assembled people.

The Plane Is On Fire!

Thanksgiving, C: Luke 17, 11-19

There is a great law of living: Shared misfortune brings people together. That is, a shared experience of misfortune will break down the natural and personal barriers among people. Let me give you an example.

I was on my way from Amman, Jordan back to the United States, and had to change planes in Paris. The jumbo jet was full as we lifted off toward the heavens, with thoughts of being home soon. Then, suddenly, there we all sat on the tarmac of the military airfield of Keflevik, Iceland. Although cold and with an uncertain future, we were laughing and drinking, sharing whatever we had, including stories of family and self. You would have thought it was a high school class reunion from all the camaraderie and intimacy of conversation.

What happened? About 435 miles off the northwest coast of Ireland, and flying at about 42,000 feet above the Arctic Ocean, the plane caught on fire. Not an external engine, but the body of the plane. It was a crisis and we were all scared. The captain told us of the severity of the danger too. He said we would fly low over the ocean but, due to the turbulence of the frigid water, would stay at least a mile above the water. If we had to crash land into the ocean, that would make for a more likely safe entry. Meanwhile, he said, they would be dumping all the fuel out of the plane, through holes at the end of each wing, in order to minimize the possibility of exploding. The nearest land mass where we might land was a military field on a peninsula on the south side of Iceland; it was about 45 minutes away. We should be calm and quiet, if possible. And we were.

When we arrived at Keflevik field, there was foam on the runway, lots of emergency equipment, and calm. We were quickly unloaded, and headed for the only building available, a small store with restrooms and one payphone. It took about 20 minutes for people to realize we were really there, safe at last, and not going to die in a fiery plane crash. Suddenly, all the people began to talk and laugh, and share. These people who sat silently with each other in the airport lounge, in the plane, now became a big family of love and support. We bought out all the food and drink - including lots of candy bars and Icelandic vodka - and gathered on the tarmac. You could hardly tell who had bought what, for everyone was sharing whatever they had with everyone else. Suddenly there was no special ownership of the food; just like the early Christian communities that we read about in the Acts of the Apostles [2:44-45]: *All who believed were together and had all things in common; they would sell their property and possessions and divide them among all according to each one's need.*

So that is how we got to be all together on the tarmac of a military airstrip in Iceland that cold summer day.

Now let us turn to consider our gospel reading. Jesus was on the border between Galilee and Samaria and was met by a band of ten lepers. We know that the Jews had no dealings with the Samaritans; yet in this band there was at least one Samaritan. We can be fairly certain that there were both men and women, young and old, and likely other tribes and nationalities among the leper colony from which they came. But here again we see an example of that great law of life: A common misfortune had broken down the racial and national barriers. In the common tragedy of their leprosy they had forgotten they were Jews and Samaritans and remembered only that they were people in need. And, in their common need, they overcame their differences.

Even wild animals behave this way. If a flood should sweep over an area, all the wild animals congregate on the high ground for safety. They stay peacefully together, even though they are animals who would normally be natural enemies and who would at other times do their best to kill and eat each other.

Surely one of the things that should draw all of humanity together is our common need to praise and thank God. But it does not work that way, it seems, except in times of trouble and difficulty. We've had a difficult year, with the tragedies in our nation and resulting war. It has, like my airplane near tragedy, like the wild animals in a flood, had an affect to bring together people who would not normally choose to be together. Out of tragedy has come this lesson - instead of building walls to define our differences, to separate ourselves in the human community from each other by class, income, race, nationality, gender, and so on, we find common bases for recognizing our shared dignity as individual people made in the image and likeness of God, endowed by our loving creator with unique gifts and talents, but sharing in the one Spirit of a Creator God who loves us, and who wants us to love each other as brothers and sisters in the same way.

Perhaps if we can overcome our tendency to focus on our differences, and see instead of common giftedness by God, we may begin to see better the many wonders of love and generosity that God has put in and among us. Perhaps then, our need and desire to thank God for all we have and are will be so compelling that we can not stop praising and thanking God for his bounteous generosity to ourselves, our families, our community, nation and world.

A blessed Thanksgiving to you.

What's It Like Over There?

11th Sunday, B: Mark 4:26-34

For many years, I traveled a lot as part of my job. It was mostly international travel, in the northern hemisphere -- Europe and Asia. Since the end of the Cold War in 1991, I have been going into the countries of the former Soviet Union and its satellites in eastern Europe. I was quite lucky – getting to go to places where most Americans had never been. So it was not uncommon, upon my return to the USA, to have my colleagues ask me "What's it like over there?" I would then show them photos, but mostly I would relate stories. And it was hard to tell people what it was like. Often it was so unlike anything I could think of, or there were so many things to describe I could not capture it all in a few words. So I would tell stories and, each story try to give an insight into the place where I had been. "It is like Montana," or "It is like the Rockies," I would say, and somehow hope that my example would be meaningful to my listeners.

Well, that is what is happening in today's gospel. The disciples of Jesus want to know what the Kingdom of God, or the Reign of God, is like. And so Jesus tells two stories to give some understanding of what it is like. It is like a growing seed which has been planted and becomes mature even if we don't notice it, and it is like a mustard seed which becomes a huge tree.

Jesus is trying to find symbols which will be familiar to his followers to make clearer what the Kingdom of God is like, and when and how they will experience it. He does not say it is like Montana, or the Rockies, or the New River Valley (maybe he could say that, however!); he says it is like the Growing Seed, and like the Mustard Seed.

The "growing seed" parable shows the contrast between the inactivity of the sower, and the certainty of the harvester. Of course, it needn't be said that they are obviously one and the same – God. The seed's growth is "irresistible" and goes on without any thought of ours. The harvest refers to the final judgment – the coming of the Kingdom of God.

It may be that this parable was Jesus' reply to those who impatiently waited for a Messiah to come and make a forceful and sudden intervention of God into the world. Jesus was telling them, that the coming will be quiet, unnoticed, but as sure as the harvest, it'll come.

It was also meant by Jesus to give assurance to those who were discouraged because nothing seemed to be happening. Jesus was preaching and teaching, miracles were occurring, but there did not seem to be much response. In spite of the apparent apathy and hindrance, the seed is being sown, Jesus says. And its growth is the work of God who will bring it to harvest. The fulfillment of the reign of God will surely come, since the seed is already planted by Jesus himself.

In the "mustard seed" parable, there is the contrast between insignificant beginnings and mighty achievement. It is not the seed itself, but what happens to the seed which is important. The seed (the Kingdom) begins small. But it will become great and mighty. In Ezekiel a tree sheltering the birds is a symbol of a great empire offering protection to all peoples – so here in Mark too the mustard "shoot" is the proclamation of the Kingdom of God intended to be for all nations.

This parable was Jesus' answer to the objection: Could the kingdom really come from such an inauspicious beginning? His reply is that the little cell of disciples will indeed become a Kingdom. And, in the final analysis, if the Kingdom does reach its full dimensions, it is not due to anything in the men and women who are the seed of the Kingdom; the growth is due solely to the power of God. That's why Jesus can speak with utter confidence of the final stage of the Kingdom. And that's why it is a call to patience.

The implications are strong for us as well. Like the disciples, we have received the seed of faith and understanding. And, like the disciples, we are able to participate in the process of the growth of the seed, that is, the Kingdom of God. We may not know when or how, or even to whom we spread the Kingdom, but we can and we do.

This means, among other things, that salvation is not something that will come at the end of our lives in death and resurrection, nor at the end of time. Salvation has already come, in and through Jesus. But salvation and faith are a process, to grow in us and in the world, just like a seed growing. Salvation occurs today, if you will let it!

But we still need to be patient for the final fulfillment of the Kingdom, with patience in

- prayer: Be constant and persevere.

- faith: A little planted in us by the word of God will grow.
- hope: in today, but also in the final coming.

Although each of us may feel insignificant as but one Christian, we are each seeds of God's plan. Like the mustard seed or the growing seed. Like the word of God planted in the first disciples, the Word of God has been planted in us, and can and will grow, by God's own plan, in his love and time.

And like the first disciples we can share in the growth of the Kingdom of God. Indeed, we must!

- Where? In ourselves, in our families, in others we touch.
- When? Anytime. Everytime.
- How? By letting God's word and love come into the world to others in and through us. In our behavior and in ourselves as role models.

But we cannot expect to see or know the results of God's work in and through us. We never know if the next person we meet is the one for whom God will use us to be the instrument of his presence.

MEDITATIONS DURING SEMINARY

"Just remember, you are not here to learn to be a seminarian. You are here to be a priest." That was a common statement in seminary when many men (and some boys!) were living in one common house, praying, studying, sharing, and experiencing all the mundane events of daily life together. It created tensions, personal stress, and communal uprising at times. It also brought much joy in shared spiritual journeys, mutual support systems, and cross-fertilized learning. Still, all in all, it was designed to be a temporary period of formation, and not a permanent condition - Thank you, Jesus.

During my four years of seminary at the Theological College and Catholic University of America, I came to much understanding about the meaning of a new life of priesthood and the loss of past possessions and friends, even a foster son as you will shortly read. Some early homilies of that time address those losses, as you will soon read. At the same time, I gained much insight into the realities that each of us can experience God, faith, and life differently, without anyone being right or wrong. One particular speaker at the seminary opened my eyes to the diversity of legitimate spiritual experiences of Jesus and of living faith in him.

Most importantly during those days of seminary, I began to see the meaning of my faith journey through preaching, initially to a Catholic grade school on a monthly basis. The homily below on the boy and the dinosaurs comes from this time. I began to recognize in others, even the oddest of people, their simultaneous call as children of God. The homily about Willy is one of those experiences.

Let us turn now to some of those reflections and homilies.

What Are You Waiting For?

2nd Sunday of Advent, B: Mark 1:1-8

All that he said to me was: "What are you waiting for?" And I could not give him a good answer, except to say I was waiting to talk with him. So there I sat in the bishop's office talking to him. Now that I had told him that I felt God wanted me to quit my job, sell my house, and go to seminary, all the Bishop could say was: "What are you waiting for?"

Well, you can see what I did in response to his question. I have waited years to stand here today, to proclaim to you by my presence what I have known in my heart for a long time - that God wants me to be his servant, that he wants to use my hands, and heart, and eyes, voice, even my mind, because he needs some help doing the work of spreading the kingdom. I have waited to learn that he accepts the offering of my life for his purpose. I have been preparing the way of the Lord for a long time. And that's what I intend to keep on doing for the rest of my life - until I see God face to face.

In last week's gospel that began our Advent season, we heard the same words that the bishop said to me: "What are you waiting for?" We are told to be watchful and wait. But, unless there is something to await, there is no reason to be watchful. Waiting implies a goal, an expectation. Waiting is not just about putting in time. Like waiting for the newspaper to come, or the toaster to pop up. That is not waiting; that is wasting time. As we began this season of Advent, the gospel challenged us with this command: Be watchful and wait. Now in this week's gospel, we learn how we are to wait - by preparing the way of the Lord. Just as John the Baptist proclaimed to the people of the Judean countryside, so too are we to prepare for Christ's coming, during our time of waiting.

So: What are you waiting for?

- For Christmas? Sorry, it already came -- two thousand years ago.

- For Jesus Christ? Sure. That's exactly right. Waiting to see Jesus again

- perhaps, when he comes again at the end of time; or for others of us,

- waiting to meet him when we die. That is what we are waiting for.

Just as Christmas commemorates and celebrates his first coming into our midst, now we await the final coming of Christ to us, at our deaths or in his return at the end.

But are we really waiting for this? Or are we just putting in time? There is quite a difference. To wait implies a goal and, therefore, a hope - a hope that when he comes, we'll be ready for the meeting -- a hope that when he comes, He will be eager to greet us.

How then do we wait for this coming of Christ into our lives again? It can be by putting in time, like waiting for the end of the workday or for the school bell to ring. Or it can be, as the gospel says, by preparing the way of the Lord; by making straight the paths of the Lord -- into our hearts and lives. The real difference between simply putting in time and preparing the way of the Lord is the difference between being passive and active.

That is the real message of the gospels of Advent. Waiting for Christ to come is not a passive activity in which we do nothing; waiting requires active and conscious preparation. Waiting for the Lord to come again, whenever, however, involves doing something to get ready, to be prepared.

Many of us are waiting for the holidays to come when we will have guests, children, grandchildren, siblings, and friends in to celebrate and share. Well, do we simply sit around and ignore the reality that they will be ringing the doorbell soon? Or do we become active in our waiting - preparing food, the house, selecting and wrapping gifts, internally and externally making ourselves ready to greet the guests when they come? We realize that waiting for something like guests takes planning and preparations. Well, so too does our gospel reading tell us to prepare actively during our watchful waiting for The Guest of Guests to enter into our hearts.

So, let me ask it again: What are you waiting for?:

- Christmas? If that means Christ's return to our hearts, then Christmas is today.

- The Christ whom we await in each death, or in his return to us at the end of time - he may also be coming today. Are you preparing? Are you prepared?

- Is there someone you need to forgive before Christ gets here? What are you waiting for?

- Is there someone who needs something you have that you can share? What are you waiting for?

- Do you know someone who can not pray, due to illness, anger, sadness, or frustration? Are you able to pray for them? What are you waiting for?
- Has God called you to do something that you are not prepared to do? Do you need the bishop to say it to you too: What are you waiting for?

Christmas is today, right here, right now. The Jesus who came 2000 years ago, is coming here today. Are you preparing? Are you prepared? If not, what are you waiting for? Christmas?

I Want To Be a Saint.

November 1, Feast of All Saints: Revelation 7:2-4, 9-14, 1 John 3:1-3, Matthew 5:1-12a

When I applied to enter seminary in February 1996, there was a series of three assignments that I had to complete as part of the application process. For one of the assignments, I had to write an essay on the question: "What is your goal in life?" Although I had plenty of paper to write, I simply took one sheet of paper and wrote six words on it, and turned it in.   I wrote: "I want to be a saint." As the final step in the application process, I had to appear before a board who had reviewed my application materials. It seems that my very short essay caught their attention. The other applicants had written many pages on their goals in life and, I guess, they were somewhat amazed by my six words. It seemed that some members of the admissions board found it a very naive and childish thing to write. When questioned about what I wrote, I told them that I had sincerely stated my goal in life - to be a saint someday.   For, as I understood the meaning of the word "saint," it referred to someone who died and was now with God for all eternity. I wanted to spend whatever time, gifts, and energies that I had, I told them, so as to make sure I can be with God forever. That seemed to satisfy the admissions board pretty well.

After four years of graduate study in preparation for priesthood, I find myself ever more sure that this is my goal in life - to be with God one day; to be a saint.

On this feast of All Saints, it is worth remembering that all those who have died and gone to be with God are saints. Some of them may be family members, friends and relatives. Some may even be enemies, people we never liked or wanted to be near here on earth. Whatever, they share in common the reality that the goals of their baptismal faith have now brought them together in love with God.

Saints are real people. The stylized, maudlin, sometimes ephemeral paintings and pictures of saints that we see in our Christian tradition are no more real images of saints than they would be of the people gathered here today. Saints come in all sizes and shapes, with all sorts of personalities.

They are not perfect as humans; it is not physical or psychological perfection which makes saints. It is the desire to serve God on earth so as to be with God eternally. They did that by being Beatitude people.

I'll say it again: Saints are real people, not storybook characters. Let me put in a word for the humanization of saints. For, only if we can imagine saints as real people just like us, can we ever imagine our very selves as possibly saints some day.

Consider these saints of our Roman calendar:

St. Jerome, scholar, biblical translator, and a thoroughly irascible and grumpy old man. He had a personality that did not win friends and admirers. But he loved God and used the gifts God had given him to serve the Church and the people of God. Fortunately, he was a "book worm" and his work did not require he spend much time with others.

Or how about St. Teresa of the Child Jesus, a shy quiet Carmelite sister of the late 19th century, who died at age 24 in a cloistered convent, with hardly any notice? But her writings, later made public, identified a heart on fire with love for God and his people, and a mystical ability to love, in humble and quiet ways. This shy quiet lady is one of the Doctors of the Church today.

St. Francis of Assisi was a simple man, not exactly the image of the statue of him that so many people put in their gardens for birds to land on, and then anoint, before departing. Francis would certainly identify with the statue after the bird's visit rather than before it!

And what about all those who have lived ordinary lives and, upon death, have found themselves happily home with God? Their names are not in our Roman calendar, but they are saints; that is, they are people who reached the goal of being with God. It is in the ordinariness of their lives that they have found extraordinariness in being just who and what God needed them to be here in this life.

Today is a good day to remember all those people who are not in any church calendar, book of saints, or religious artwork, but who are saints too. Maybe some in particular have touched your life -- grandparents, parents, teachers, friends, even spouses and children. They too are among the saints of God! Let us ask them to pray for us, so that one day we may join them.

[Whenever I have the opportunity to be with people as they are dying I say: "If you get there before I do, please tell God of my love for Him, of my gratitude to Him. Pray for me that one day I might join you." That may sound strange but there is a comfort in a dying person knowing that soon they be able to intercede for others who are waiting for their own sainthood someday.]

As we honor all those who have gone before us to return to be with our God, may we too have the courage to seek to become saints one day. Let us give thanks for everyone in heaven whom we love and who love us.

Giving Up Career and Possessions

22nd Sunday, A: Jeremiah 20:7-9, Romans 12:1-2, Matthew 16:21-27

Jesus says we will save our lives by losing them. The point is that sacrifice and suffering for the fervent Christian are not likelihoods; they are inevitable, indeed they are a necessity.

When I announced that I was giving up my career and home and going to seminary in spring 1996, many of my friends and most of my professional colleagues were aghast at my decision. They thought I was crazy. "How could you give up a lucrative job, the opportunity to travel around the world so much, and, most of all, your home at the country club, your furniture and collections, and all the material objects collected from around the world?" "Why would you do something so stupid?" they asked. My replies were two and they were simple:

- Yes, it is hard to give up the career, travel and material things. But I no longer need any of them as a seminarian, then a deacon and a priest.
- While it may be a bit difficult to give all this up, it is even more difficult to resist God's summons to become a priest.

In a nutshell, it is easier to give up my past life than to say NO to God. So I said YES to God and moved on. That is essentially what Jeremiah, in our first reading, had to do, only his sacrifice was a thousand-fold greater than mine could ever be. He had to risk family, life and limb, in order to say YES to God's invitation to be a prophet of the Lord. He did not like it at times, he tried to tell the Lord to find someone else. But he had to say YES; he liked even less the refusal of God's call to serve.

The story from Jeremiah is meant to explain what Jesus means in the gospel today when he speaks of saving our lives by losing them. Jeremiah is depressed, really depressed. Yet, on the other hand, there is something else happening, even as Jeremiah sinks to his lowest level. It is the strong and clear conviction that he has no real choice in the matter. God's call to prophecy is a consuming fire for him, and even though obeying it brings suffering, obedience is not a matter of choice. Thus we see the fervor of Jeremiah's discipleship as well as the depth of his suffering. He can endure his sacrifice and suffering far more easily than he can resist the summons to speak on God's behalf.

If you were able to pay close attention to the first reading, you noticed, perhaps, that Jeremiah's entire address is actually a prayer, but he addresses it to God in the second and third person. It begins: *You duped me, O LORD, and I let myself be duped; you were too strong for me, and you triumphed.* (Jeremiah 20:7) Jeremiah is indirect and is unable to look at God and say these things. Jeremiah does not want to do the Lord's work and he says so: *I say to myself, I will not mention him, I will speak in his name no more.* *But then it becomes like fire burning in my heart, imprisoned in my bones; I grow weary holding it in, I cannot endure it.* (Jeremiah 20:9) But Jeremiah also admits that he can't stop himself from obeying the Lord. Who of us can use these words with sincerity. Who among us can tell the Lord that we don't like what he has in mind for us, that we don't want to use the gifts we have received to do the work of the Lord? Most of us can not tell this to the Lord in our words, so we simply do it by our actions, or, more correctly, by our inactions. We don't say NO to God directly, we let our inactions do the talking.

Now let's look at the gospel. Now we are about at the midpoint of Matthew's gospel and Jesus begins to alter dramatically the apostles' understanding of who Jesus is and what he came to do. *Jesus began to show his disciples that he must go to Jerusalem and suffer greatly ..., and be killed and on the third day be raised.* (Matthew 16:21) Peter's horrified response is perfectly understandable, but he is about to hear even more painful news. Jesus will achieve our salvation in a far different way than what generations of faithful Jews expected the Messiah to do. He won't be a conquering warrior; he won't restore the kingdoms of Israel; and he won't trample Israel's enemies. Instead, he will die for his people, as a total act of self-giving. He will conquer death, and so save all, and open the doors of heaven to all who can follow him through this life and onto eternal life. Got that, Peter: You too must give all for my sake!

To Peter, this sounds like a defeat, a sure disgrace for Jesus. And, in earthly terms, I guess it was. How can Jesus claim to be the Messiah, and then die at the hands of enemies? It is unthinkable that the Messiah should sacrifice, suffer, die. Simply unthinkable. So Jesus speaks on.

God's ways are at work here, not human ways. Clinging to earthly things, even earthly life, is not God's way. Spending our life, using up our gifts, our strength, ourselves, for the sake of others - that is the way of

God. But it won't be understood by the disciples until Easter morning.

But you who sit here on this (Saturday evening) Sunday morning. You already know about Easter morning, just as you know about Jesus' selfless acts of love. Why is it that you still cling to the things of this life, to your material things, as somehow your own, and not strive to expend them for others? Why is it that you do not see that sacrifice and suffering for the fervent Christian are not likelihoods?- that they are inevitable, indeed they are a necessity.

The old saying: "You can't take it with you" applies, not just to our material goods; it applies to our talents, our psychological and intellectual gifts as well. So spend them now, on earth, before you die - on doing the work which Jesus has given you to do to build up his kingdom. You can't take it with you!

What profit would there be for one to gain the whole world and forfeit his life? (Matthew 16:26)

We Have All Been Called.

25th Sunday, A: Isaiah 55:6-9, Matthew 20:1-16a

Seek the LORD while he may be found, call him while he is near. (Isaiah 55:6). That is the first line of today's first reading from Isaiah. That is the point of the readings today - to actively and aggressively seek the Lord - by responding to his call to work for God's harvest.

When you listen to the gospel, you may not get that idea. The parable of the generous landowner remains a mystery to us if we conclude that what the workers were given was some "thing." The parable takes on a different meaning if the payment is Someone. After all, this is not a parable about just wages; it is about the kingdom of heaven. Recall how Jesus begins this parable: *The kingdom of heaven is like a landowner who went out at dawn ....* (Matthew 20:1).

God's goodness to us is made apparent. The landowner is meant to symbolize God, and the workers who are called and respond are those who hear the word of Jesus and answer, going into the world to help Jesus reap a harvest of many people for the kingdom of heaven.

The landowner does two things: He calls people into his vineyard to work for him, and he pays the workers at the end of the day. Regarding the payment of the workers, we observe that all who labor for the fullness of the kingdom can expect the same: They can expect to be given lovingly into the embrace of God, eternally. Whether one has worked a lifetime, or only for a short while, all receive much more than one could ever hope for or expect! It is not that some of the workers did not get enough; it is that all got so much more than they could have ever expected to have on their own. They got Jesus, joy and peace eternally.

The landowner's other activity - calling the workers into the vineyard - moves the focus from the generous landowner to the workers. It is they who respond to the call of the landowner to go out and work, to do what they can. Now, if the landowner symbolizes God, then whom are we intended to see in the workers, standing around in the market? They are, of course, all of us. We are the ones whom God is calling into his harvest. It is we whom God needs to do his work.

Some people, like some of the workers in the gospel, are called early, and they have the opportunity to serve God's kingdom all their lives. Others, like many of us, may be called but we don't respond right away. Who knows why? Perhaps we aren't listening, or we don't recognize the voice calling us as from God. It does not make a difference now. What does matter is that we do hear at last, and, in hearing and understanding God's call, we respond with our YES. We agree to go out into the vineyards of the kingdom of heaven, and help do the work of which Jesus asks of us. At issue is not who hears or when they hear; it is about a loving God calling out repeatedly so that eventually all will hear and respond.

With that said, then what is the appropriate response to God? It is to go into the field and use our God-given talents, whatever they are, to build up the kingdom.

Now let's bring that understanding down to the level of our parish and us as the members and workers of that parish. The call to go into the harvest for Jesus and reap the kingdom is a call to all of us to offer ourselves to God in the service of the community here at Sacred Heart Church, and in the Danville area.

If you have already heard the Master call and have responded, that is good. But you still need to listen to see if you are being called to serve in more ways, or in different ways. If you are still listening, and have not heard the call to work, or have heard it and not responded, now is the time to *Seek the LORD while he may be found, call him while he is near*, as it was said in Isaiah (55:6).

Next weekend is our Time and Talent Stewardship Sunday, a time for all of our members to decide how and where they will share their time and talents to build up the community of our parish. At each Mass next weekend there will be tables in the Commons, describing the many different ways you can serve in the parish. Please plan to stop by, and find your particular calling to serve. Please pray at this Mass and throughout the week, asking to hear the Lord and guide you in responding to His call to service.

There are needs for you and your gifts. Some are short-term and occasional; others ask for ongoing commitment of service. Some are easy and some require training. Whatever you can share of your time and talents, there is a place for you. We need Eucharistic ministers for Mass and homebound, servers, lectors, greeters and ushers, nursery staffing, children's liturgy leaders, musicians, choir members, and so much more. We want to develop a children's choir, a youth band, a parish nursing program, and a social justice committee. Let us know your gift which God is calling you to share. There is a place for it and you.

Do it, not because you need to, not because you think you can earn something from God, not out of fear, or pressure, or guilt. Do it in thanksgiving to the God who has given you all, whose Son has asked you to go out and help with the harvest of the Kingdom. Do it out of love, with joy, and eagerness.

There is Someone who needs you. You might just find that Someone in service to the Kingdom.

They Won't Let Me Wash Their Feet.

Holy Thursday: Supper of the Lord: John 13:1-15

When I went to seminary in Washington, DC, four years ago, I began on my own to go outside with plastic bags from the store, and to pick up the trash that was always abundant in the lawns of Theological College. Many of the seminarians made fun of me for doing this, saying it was not proper for a seminarian to do such a menial thing. Soon I became an object of teasing about my regular activity of picking up garbage. Word got to the faculty there and I was called in and asked to explain why I did this lawn cleaning. My answer was simply this: "I pick up the trash because you won't let me wash your feet." And I meant it too.

We read in today's gospel of the washing of the feet of the Twelve by Jesus. Jesus even washed the feet of Judas Iscariot, his betrayer. But why do we read the story of the foot-washing on Holy Thursday, instead of the Institution of the Eucharist? Most people think of the Eucharistic institution when they think of this solemn holy evening. In answer, washing the feet of others shows all who follow Christ what they are to do, as a result of Jesus' gift of his Body and Blood.

At the Last Supper, Jesus gave himself to others in the bread and wine. But here in John's Gospel, the wonderful story of the first Eucharist is not to be found. Instead, this gospel tells of the Passover Meal of Jesus and the Twelve, in which Jesus gives himself for the service of others as exemplified by the washing of his disciples' feet. Then, on the next day, Jesus shows the extent to which he gives himself for others - on the cross, unto death, out of complete love for us.

The foot-washing by Jesus and the institution of the Eucharist are closely related. If we want to be like Jesus and follow him as a disciple, we take his body and blood into ourselves, just as the Twelve did and, strengthened by his presence within us, we serve others in humility, as the foot washing demonstrates.

Would you have let Jesus wash your feet? If you are like me and most other people, I'll bet you would be like Peter and say No. Maybe because you feel unworthy; maybe because you are too proud to do such a humiliating thing. Would it be your humility or your pride which would be your consideration in deciding whether to let your feet be washed?

Jesus washed Peter's feet, and he told Peter that he could not share in the inheritance with Jesus if he did not let Jesus wash his feet. It seems to me that, by implication, Jesus is saying that all who want to be his disciples must let Jesus wash their feet. That is, we must let Jesus serve us, just as he served the Twelve. Just like he served so many others in his life and work of his Father. But how do we let Jesus wash our feet? How do we let him serve us?

- By acknowledging our need for him in all we do;

- By asking for His grace and aid in our journey to grow to join him with his Father;

- By admitting that we can do nothing without his help.

Jesus serves us too, washes our feet, when he gives us himself in the Eucharist. This is an act of Jesus' loving service to each of us; it reminds us of the ultimate gift of love for us which we will recall tomorrow on Good Friday. But the Eucharistic Gift of Jesus to us is not an end in and of itself; it is a means to help us to follow Jesus, and become like Jesus. When Jesus gave us the gift of himself on that first Holy Thursday evening, he showed us what we are to do and be, as a result of his gift of Body and Blood. The Gospel of John makes it very explicit - Jesus' gift to us on Holy Thursday was showing us how we are to be his disciples. It is through humble service to all the men and women for whom Jesus died, that we continue to do his work of salvation. It is in serving others that we celebrate the gift of his new life of the Eucharist within us.

In five weeks, by the grace of God and with your support and prayers, I will be ordained as a priest of Christ. I hope you will be able to join me on that day, and for my first Mass here at St. Benedict's. If you do, you will receive a holy card, with my name and the dates and places of my ordination and first Mass. Please pause and consider what is the picture on the front of that holy card. It is a painting of Jesus washing the feet of his disciples. I took the Last Supper example of Jesus in John's Gospel to heart many years ago. Jesus says we are all called to be his disciples, not just the ordained, and he showed us that, just as he gave us the wonderful Eucharistic gift of himself, we too are to give ourselves to others.

Please let Jesus wash your feet.

Please wash others' feet like Jesus did.

We Want to Be Like Jesus.

6th Week, Thursday, I: Mark 8: 27-35

We want to be like Jesus; that's what we pray for and that is what we prepare for here at Theological College.

Sometimes our prayer is a bit like the golden touch of King Midas. When he got his wish that everything he touched might turn to gold, he did not realize the implications of getting what he asked for. Our prayers can be that way sometimes, especially if we do not realize what we are saying when we pray.

We want to be like Jesus, we pray. But do we really mean it? Or do we mean that we want to be like some aspects of Jesus, but not others?

Jesus preached and taught, and received the accolades and praise of the people. We want to be like that.

Jesus healed and helped so many, and won the admiration and honor of the people. We want to be like that.

Jesus put on fine clothes and rode into Jerusalem to the loving worship of the crowds. We want to be like that.

Jesus got down on the floor and washed his disciples' feet. We want to be like that? Don't we?

Jesus was insulted, spat upon, whipped and persecuted? We want to be like that? We do, don't we?

Jesus carried his cross, suffered incredibly for others, and died a lonely death so that he might bring others the promise of resurrection? Do we want to be like that?

In the gospel reading, Peter recognized Jesus as the Messiah, but he recognized the Messiah, not as Jesus was, but as Peter wanted the Messiah to be - a kingly, powerful leader, a person who would be admired, put on a pedestal, and treated as one above the common and mundane of the "regular people."

Peter wanted to be like Jesus too. That is, Peter wanted to be like the Messiah he had envisioned before he met Jesus, the Messiah. Peter judged Jesus by human standards, not by God's and, in remonstrating Jesus, he was tempting Jesus to become that kind of earthly and kingly Messiah. Jesus overcame the temptation with the words: *Get behind me, Satan!* (Mark 8:33)

As seminarians we too are tempted to become the Messiah-priest of Peter's standards. Some invite us to put on the robes of honor, to parade in the accolades of self-importance and honor among our earthly brothers and sisters.

But we pray "We want to be like Jesus." Do we know what we are saying when we pray in those words? Like King Midas who got what he asked for, we too might get what we ask of Jesus if we are not careful. And the consequences of having our prayers accepted may mean our acceptance of a broader role as instruments of the Kingdom.

[Prayer]: Lord, make us priests and ministers by God's standards. Choose us as you chose the disciples, use us as your power and action in the world, and send us, Lord to the nations to proclaim your Kingdom - by our words, by our actions, by our living and our daily dying to self.

Accept us as you accept these gifts we are about to offer.

The Death of My Foster Son

24th Sunday, A: Sirach 27:30–28:9, Romans 14:7-9, Matthew 18:21-35

One must forgive in order to be forgiven. That's not so difficult to understand. It occurs throughout Jesus' teachings. One who can't forgive others can't hope that God will forgive him. *Blessed are the merciful, said Jesus, for they shall obtain mercy.* (Matthew 5:7). No sooner had Jesus taught his disciples his own prayer with the words *Forgive us our trespasses as we forgive those who trespass against us,* than he went on to expand and explain that one petition in the prayer. Jesus said, *For if you forgive others their trespasses, your heavenly father also will forgive you; but if you do not forgive others their trespasses, neither will your Father forgive your trespasses* (Matthew 6:14,15). In our first reading, it is worded this way: *Forgive your neighbor's injustice; then when you pray, your own sins will be forgiven.* (Sirach 28:2)

The point is extremely clear: Divine and human forgiveness go hand in hand. Why is this so? That too is clear: Nothing we have to forgive others can even faintly compare with what we have been forgiven by our loving God. We have been forgiven a debt which is beyond all paying - the sin of all people brought about the death of God's own Son - and God has forgiven us. So, we must forgive others as God has forgiven us, or we can hope to find no mercy.

I suspect you are sitting there and thinking that this sounds wonderful and that it takes no great mind to understand that we must forgive others, that God has forgiven us, and that not to forgive others is the same as telling God we don't need to be forgiven ourselves. Fine words indeed. Easy to understand. Nearly impossible to follow, however. This is one of Jesus' teachings that we simply wish he would not have taught. It is just too hard for forgive! Yes, I agree. Forgiveness is hard. But non-forgiveness is even harder, I would contend. When the heart is full of anger or hatred for someone, when it is most difficult to forgive someone else, the heart grows cold and callous. It is a truism of nature that, when the heart is full of a negative feeling, there is no room for good feelings. When one is full of unforgiveness, it eats at the heart, fills the mind, and makes it impossible to grow in love. To my way to thinking, hating, anger, unforgiveness are a waste of time - they get us nothing, they remove all positive feelings such as love and kindness, gentleness and joy, and they waste a lot of mental time and energy. It takes too much effort to hate, not to forgive. Personally, I have better things to do with my time, my mind and my heart. I refuse to let someone pull me down into unforgiveness, hatred, or anger. I don't deserve it, and I won't let it happen. So, aside from what Jesus teaches about forgiveness, at a very practical level, unforgiveness is a waste of time and energy. I deserve to give myself something better than feelings of unforgiveness. So I won't let someone else control me by causing me not to forgive them.

If you find that kind of thinking strange, let me tell you some personal examples. First, as a teenager, many kids made much fun of me as a teen because of my being so fat and egg-headed. I wasted much of my teen years trying to overcome their meanness to me; I let their cruelty to me subsume me, waste my time and energy. When, in late high school, I simply said, I forgive them, I put it behind me. Then I began to grow as a person. Today, none would ever know of those years of teasing if I did not tell them.

Another example. Nearly five years ago my foster son was murdered. I will tell you about that sometime. One of the worst moments of my life occurred when I had to go to the wake and funeral, with full knowledge that his killers would also be there. They thought no one knew who did the crime, so came to the funeral, took my hand, expressed their sorrow, not knowing I knew what they had done. No one can tell me about hatred and anger; no one can know what that felt like. But it was a short-lived feeling. Because such strong feelings of unforgiveness were eating me alive; I could not grow, I could not feel joy. So, I did what I had to do. I did what Jesus asked in today's gospel. I forgave his killers. I simply forgave them, and I prayed that they' feel sorrow and ask God's forgiveness too. I prayed that God would forgive them too. Then the feelings of hatred went away. Whatever else, forgiveness brings peace of mind.

One final comment. There is only one person who could even forgive instantly. And that was Jesus when he walked the earth. For all the rest of us, forgiveness is a process. It is a process that can take a lifetime to accomplish. And the process begins with the desire to forgive, even if there is no real ability to forgive.

In just a few minutes we will stand and repeat the words which Jesus gave us. We'll all have the opportunity to say: *Forgive us our debts as we forgive our debtors.* (Matthew 6:12) Before you say those words, think carefully what you are saying. Pause now and reflect. Do you want God to be just as forgiving as you are, or do you expect God to forgive you more and better than you can forgive others? Be careful what you answer; be careful what you pray!

Now, consider for a moment your own life. If there is someone who you have not forgiven, whom it is difficult to forgive? Maybe it is a former spouse who hurt you. Maybe it is a parent who abused you, or did not love you. Maybe it is a former friend who betrayed you. Whoever it is, forgive them. Not because they deserve forgiveness, not because you love them, but because Jesus forgives you, and them, and anyone who comes to him with a sincere heart, full of forgiveness of others.

Forgive yourself too for the wrongs you may have done. And then let the Lord forgive you anew. Come then to this altar, having said the words of Jesus: *Forgive us our trespasses as we forgive those who trespass against us.* Know well the peace of forgiveness, know well the peace of being forgiven.

The Scholar at Seminary, and the Death of Jesus

14th Sunday, A: Zechariah 9:9-10, Romans 8:9, 11-13, Matthew 11:25-30

In the Gospel we're invited to accept the yoke and burden of Christ. He tells us that the yoke is easy and the burden light. I don't think that many people really believe these words of Jesus, however. This easy yoke and light burden means our submission to God's will. Submitting to the will of God stands in sharp contrast to our desire to following our own will, our own needs and desires - that is, to be in control. But it's Christ's yoke and burden which is light; it is our own self-imposed burdens which are the heavy burden and difficult yoke.

Even our desires to please God can be a burdensome and weary yoke that far exceeds Christ's burden, a burden that He says is easy and light. Do I find the yoke of Christ easy? The burden of Christ light? Or is it difficult and wearisome? Do I add so much to the yoke and burden of Christ that it becomes too hard for me? Is it Christ's burden, or Christ's, plus my own self-imposed burden that is heavy and difficult?

A yoke is not meant to be a burden, but a guide. The yoke of an animal is something that provides discipline and direction to the animal so yoked. For the Jews in the time of Christ, their yoke was the Law of Moses, given by God to show the people how to live in a covenant relationship with God. It was meant to be a joy to know God's will. But the religious sect, the Pharisees, had added more than 200 additional rules to the Law by the time of Jesus, so that this gift of the Law was no longer a joy, but a burden and difficult. And, Jesus railed against the Pharisees for adding so many extra requirements to the Law. Jesus criticized them and accused them for using these extra requirements as ways for them to show off their religiousness, with public displays of what they thought were pious rituals. We still have our modern-day Pharisees today, but now they are "Christian Pharisees" who can make the burden of Christ's yoke wearisome and difficult.

Once at a meeting at my old seminary, a noted biblical scholar gave us seminarians an assignment. He said that he wanted us to reflect on the meaning of the passion and death of Jesus. After a few minutes of silent reflection, we were to form into small groups and share how Christ's passion and death gave insight and meaning to each of our lives. What happened in these small groups was amazing. There were two very distinct understandings of Christ's passion and death. One group understood the spiritual meaning of Christ's passion and death as an example of overcoming suffering and difficulty and, for that group, a key spiritual notion was perseverance and endurance of suffering. The other group understood Christ's passion and death principally as an example of perfect love, of Christ's complete gift of his life for the love of others. For this group, the important spiritual notion was conforming one's life to the unselfish love of Christ.

Now, of course, both groups were insightful in finding a spiritual meaning that they could relate to their lives. And both understandings were appropriate for any Christian. But, in the discussion that followed, the two groups began to examine why they thought so differently. What we learned was this.

The first group which focused on Christ's passion as an example of overcoming suffering and difficulty was made up of guys who saw life more pessimistically, as something to be endured and eventually overcome in dying to eternal life. The other group, which understood Christ's passion and dying as an example of perfect love, was made up of guys who experienced life more optimistically, with the opportunity to seek and find Christ's presence just as much in this world as in the eternal life to come. For the former, the yoke of Christ was hard; for the latter, it was light.

What may account for this difference in focus? Let us consider some aspects of our Christian acceptance of Christ's burden and yoke, and how we might make the burden difficult and the yoke heavy.

First, for some there is a strong sense of guilt, a feeling that is common to all who are aware of their sinfulness. But strong feelings of guilt can make us weary, can burden us down, even overpower us into depression. They also ignore God's genuine forgiveness.

Second, for many, a sense of unworthiness of God's love can be very strong too. We are not worthy of God's love, and we cannot deserve all that God gives us in his bounteous and gracious goodness. Of ourselves, we can never be worthy of God's love. But we don't have to be; Jesus made us worthy by what he did for us. He justified us by his life and death, and he made us righteous before God. What we can not do for ourselves, Christ has done for us. As Paul wrote in his letter to the Romans:

If the Spirit of the one who raised Jesus from the dead dwells in you, the one who raised Christ from the dead will give life to your mortal bodies also, through his Spirit that dwells in you. (Romans 8:11).

If we don't believe that Jesus has done this for us, we may be tempted to try to earn God's love. But that is impossible. More than that, it is an act of disbelief in the work and meaning of Christ's life and death. The point of all this is: We do not have to make the yoke of Christ burdensome and weary. That yoke is submission to the will of the Father, not to our own feelings of guilt or unworthiness, not to our own needs to prove our worthiness to ourselves and others by excessive and public acts of piety, not by being over-zealous Pharisees.

Finally, in addition to guilt and the sense of unworthiness, we can make the yoke and burden of Christ more difficult by our own pride, our egos, which lead us to think we know what is good, right, proper, and correct, even more so that does the gospel, the Church or its teachers and leaders. However, our first reading today reminds of the coming of a messiah who is meek and humble. And our gospel affirms us in Jesus' own words that He is meek and humble of heart. (Matthew 11:29) It is by imitation of the humility of Christ that we put on Christ's yoke. It is not by becoming a proud Pharisee with lots of extra rules, imposed on ourselves and others, that we imitate Christ. It is tempting to think we have had personal revelation and know what is best and right - for ourselves and for everyone else too. But there isn't personal revelation; Jesus Christ was the ultimate, complete and final revelation. To think otherwise is pride - eating of the fruit of the tree in the center of the Garden of Eden, as Genesis records - and this pride can make the easy yoke and light burden of Christ into an arrogant self-righteousness for some, and a weary and difficult burden for others.

So, in today's readings we are challenged to examine ourselves to see how we experience our lives as Christians. Is life a burden to be overcome with perseverance, or an opportunity to experience Christ with joy and anticipation? What does our understanding of how we confront life tell us about how we put on the yoke and burden of Christ? How does this affect how we encounter Christ in our lives, in our prayers, in our heart?

Willy in Waverly

13th Sunday, A: 2 Kings 4:8-11, 14-16a, Romans 6:3-4, 8-11, Matthew 10:37-42

If you don't know what you are looking at, there's not much point in keeping your eyes open, is there?   That's the way it is with prophets. There could be one right in front of you, and you wouldn't know it. So how could you offer him or her a cup of cold water to drink, like Jesus asks us to do?

Jesus tells us that recognition is the key to reward. We have to look for the prophets and disciples around us, and we have to welcome them abundantly. I guess we all need to go out looking for the prophets in the world and then make them welcome. At least that is what these readings seem to tell us.

There are two issues here. Recognizing a prophet in our midst, and then welcoming the prophet appropriately. Let's consider each of these tasks.

How do we recognize a prophet? A prophet is someone whom God chooses to speak words in behalf of God himself. Prophets give their voices and actions into the Lord's care, and let God use themselves as instruments to serve God in the world. It takes courage for a prophet to let God do that. And many have tried to say no. (Consider Jeremiah and Jonah, for example.) But those who let God use them become people whose actions and words are not their own, but those of God himself.

In our first reading we have this warm and touching story of hospitality and gratitude. Both the woman's generosity and the prophet's kindness in return are examples of graciousness. The compilers of the lectionary obviously chose this text because it exemplifies what Jesus says in today's gospel reading: Whoever welcomes a prophet is rewarded accordingly. This generous woman demonstrates how one can recognize the gift of a prophet in our midst. It is in Elisha's words and actions that she recognizes the presence of God. And her recognition does not depend on the content of the prophet's message. No matter if the words of the prophet are something we want to hear or something we fear, the prophet is to be welcomed. The prophet's role is to speak for God.   Whether the message is one of warning or comfort , or both, the prophet must proclaim it courageously.

So where are today's prophets? Our second reading provides the answer. Speaking to anyone who has been baptized, Paul wrote: ... *you too must think of yourselves as dead to sin and living for God in Christ Jesus.* (Romans 6:11) We are all prophets if we let God use us as instruments of his good news in the world. We are all chosen to be visible and tangible signs of what Jesus taught and did, and then sent his own disciples to do.

The implications of this admission (if you can admit that you are a prophet and disciple) are amazing. First, it means that you will consciously try to recognize in others around you the possibility of God's actions and words in their lives - actions and words possibly directed toward you, given by God to you, through those about you.

Second, you have to accept the possibility that your own words and actions are signs for others of God's presence in the world, that there are people in your life, your family, your workplace, who depend on you to be an expression of God in their world.

Thirdly, and probably the most difficult, you have to welcome others with generous hospitality, no matter their message and appearance, as potential prophets of Jesus in our world today. That's not something easy to do. Most of us are so quick to judge people by first impressions that we've closed our minds to the possibility of their being someone chosen by God, long before they can say a word or do a thing! Do you ever wonder how many times and in how many ways God has tried to speak to you, to help you, to love you, to give to you, but you did not listen, did not pay attention, just because the messenger did not look the way you wanted? Because the messenger was someone whom you pre-judged as not part of your crowd?

It works the other way around too. How many people are missing the experience of the Christ in you because they had determined ahead of time that you were not someone worth knowing, hearing, and experiencing?

Time for a story. Let me tell you about Willy, but that may not be his real name. Since he is mentally retarded and has no teeth, it is hard to understand his speech. He's called "the village idiot" in Waverly, Virginia, a village of about 2600 people, where I used to work in outreach ministry. Whatever else you might say about Willy, you cannot deny that he is genuinely ugly, deformed, and hard to look at. And, despite his limited intelligence, Willy knows what it is like to be known as someone hard to look at. Each morning Willy gets up and dresses himself, putting on the stub of each leg, just below the knee joint, a tennis shoe. He puts them on backwards, with the toes pointing backward, tying the laces behind what were once his knees. Then he begins to walk about on his partial legs, with the confidence that the padded sneakers give him.

Willy is quite short due to the loss of his lower legs, but still he puts himself to work everyday. He has an old grocery-store shopping cart, which he keeps on the back porch of the group home where he lives at the corner of Coppahaunk and Main. The cart contains a broom, a rake, some plastic shopping bags, and other miscellaneous cleaning items. Right after breakfast each day, Willy starts out into his limited neighborhood, pushing the shopping cart which is nearly as high as he is. He cleans the lawn and sidewalk around his home, then along the streets. Next he crosses the street to the nursery school and cleans around it, and finally goes cater-corner to another home to clean the yard and sidewalk and street.

Willy is trying to make the world more beautiful. He knows what it is like not to have beauty, so he does what he can, with the limited mental and physical capacity he has, to make what God has created more beautiful.

I've talked with his neighbors. Some can understand him when he talks. He says that he is asking God to make all things beautiful again. He knows about loss of beauty, and he knows that Jesus made a lost humanity beautiful again. He just wants to help. Willy would wash people's feet if they would let him; he just wants to be more like Jesus. So he does what he can to follow in Jesus' model. Who knows? Jesus says we must love no one and nothing more than himself. Maybe Willy would love father or mother, brother or sister, more than Jesus if he had any family. But he does not. So with his simple acts of love, coming out of his very hard-to-look at humanity, Willy is serving God's creatures with the gifts he has been given. And he hopes that he too can receive a *prophet's reward*, just as Jesus promised in our gospel today - which, I suppose, Willy would think of as trading his human body for a heavenly and beautiful one some day.

Willy is not able to understand that, in this daily acts of love for God's creation, he has made himself beautiful too. Willy is unaware that he makes Christ visible for others. Willy does not know that others think him beautiful in what he does. Willy does not know that he is a prophet of the Lord for others, at least for those who let themselves get close enough to Willy to experience him.

But we can understand that we make ourselves beautiful before God and others in our words and deeds. We know that we can recognize God as acting in us and others when we do as Jesus did. We can understand that we have a prophet's reward waiting for us.

Now we all have the opportunity to do what Jesus did by his life and death. We all have the opportunity to be prophets, to show by our words and actions the faith which Jesus promised us would give us a prophet's reward. We can recognize God in our midst, can't we?

If a guy like Willy, walking around on stubs with backward-sneakers on, can be Christ-like, maybe we can all commit ourselves today to make some small part of our lives, our families, our environment beautiful again. If we can look beyond the outer appearance of others, we may see God in others, waiting to awaken our faith to action.

If you can see God in others, maybe then someone will recognize God in you, as many do in Willy. Just as the disciples were at last able to do, in Jesus.

One final question: If you passed little Willy on the street, would you give him a cup of cold water to drink??

The Little Boy and Dinosaurs

2nd Sunday of Lent, B: Mark 9:2-10

God gives his Son to the world - an act of divine Love.

God shows his Son to be the beloved Son - an act of divine Love.

Christ goes to the Cross and dies for us - an act of divine Love.

Christ shows his Spirit to be with and in us - an act of divine Love.

Sometimes I wonder just how different Jesus looked at the moment of his Transfiguration, about which we just read in the gospel. Was it that Jesus changed so much, to radiate in his glory? Or was it that the three disciples were at last able to see some of what was always present in Jesus - a divine love radiating out in his teaching and his actions of serving others? Personally, I think it was both. Which brings me to the point of my reflection: To what extent do we let the Christ that is in each of us, by virtue of our Baptisms, be seen by others? To what extent do we look beyond the outer trappings of others to see the Christ in them?

Both questions are reflective of the same phenomenon, and it can be stated simply: Christ is in us. We say it like this:

- In our baptisms and confirmations, we receive the Holy Spirit;
- At Eucharist we receive the Body and Blood of Christ;
- When we hear the Word of God proclaimed and preached, we receive Christ; and
- We are each temples of the Holy Spirit.

Now, if we can believe any one of these statements, then we acknowledge the Christ-presence in every one of us gathered here. So: You are standing in the presence of the glorified Lord, just as were the three disciples in our gospel reading today! That is a fact. It is that simple.

Christ, the one who was transfigured;

Christ, the one who suffered and died nearly 2000 years ago,

Christ, the one we pray to, praise, thank, and honor,

Christ, our Lord, our God, our best friend - He is present within you, he is beside you today, in those gathered here. It is awesome! BUT we don't seem awed! We are not impressed! We don't seem to believe it or, if you do, you don't seem to care.

We are like so many who, when confronted with the reality of Christ among us, just as present as he was in his Transfiguration, do not have a reaction. Why not? Let me suggest that the reason is that we have all been conditioned to disbelieve the reality of Christ's presence in us. As we have grown to maturity, we've been conditioned to ignore the reality of the inpouring of the Holy Spirit in us in the sacraments, in the liturgy, in our prayers and our times of need. We have become too sophisticated to be awed by anything.

Jesus was right when he preached that, unless we become like little children again, we cannot enter the kingdom of God. For it is little children who seem to be open to the mystery of life, accepting of the love of God, and not yet made callous to love, or conditioned by peer pressure, secular standards, machismo, or other influences to ignore the beautiful mystery of God as real.

A couple of years ago I was invited to preach a grade school Mass where I worked in Maryland. The kids were pre-K through eighth grade, and the Gospel was Jesus teaching his disciples to pray the "Our Father." I wanted to preach about how very personal God must be since Jesus told us to address God as "Our Father." I started my homily to the children with the words: "I have never been to heaven but I would like to think that God has a refrigerator up there, and that he has a picture on the front of that refrigerator which you drew." I thought the kids could relate to that image, and begin to see God as a loving and proud parent. Well, I had hardly gotten out the phrase "I have never been to heaven, but I'd like to think ...." when a first grade boy raised his hand and started to squirm and wave at me. It caught my attention, and so I stopped, walked down the aisle to him, and squatted down beside him at his pew. When I asked him what he wanted to say, he replied: "You've never been to heaven??? Well, I know what heaven is like and what God has there." I put my hand over my microphone discretely, just in case, and asked him what he knew. With pride and assurance he told me: "That is where all the dinosaurs are!" The other kids nearby laughed at this, but I quieted them down and turned back to my first grader. [Now I was covering my microphone tightly!] "Why," I asked him, "are all the dinosaurs in heaven with God?" And his immediate reply was: "They must be there because they are not here. God made them, and God loves everything he has made. If they aren't here, it must be that he took them all back home to be with him."

Imagine. I thought I was going to teach these children about a God who is loving and real!!! The wisdom and beauty of a child - no masks, no pretense -- seeing God just as God is intended to be seen!!!

As we prepare for Easter, let's take off the masks we wear, and let others see Christ in us. Let's get rid of the garbage we have put on since our baptisms - the macho, the secular, the blase, the too-cool attitudes toward self and our religion, so that others might see in us the God who is our creator, our savior, our friend, and our goal.

If you are not sure how to do that, just turn and ask Him how. He is right here beside you, not transfigured in his glory as in the gospels, but transformed in the baptized people about you. I dare you to ask Him. I challenge you to find Christ in someone today. I challenge you even more strongly to let Him be seen in you. Today.

Who Comforts the Comforter? The Death of Kevin

2nd Sunday of Lent, C: Luke 9:28b-36

Whenever there is a crisis, someone has to take on the role of the strong-shoulders-to-lean-on.   Invariably it is the same person who becomes that Rock of Gibraltar.

In our gospel Jesus is on his way to Jerusalem, and there he'll undergo much suffering and be crucified. Jesus knew that his disciples would be scared, really terrified, and so Jesus did what he did so many times before. He took onto his shoulders the burdens and fears of others, so that they may be able to endure what was to come. Jesus became the strong one again, this time for Peter and Andrew, for James and John. So that they might be able to endure his soon-to-occur suffering and death and, in turn, so that they would be able to endure their own sufferings and deaths, Jesus showed them who he was. He transfigured himself before them, from his human self to his glorified self as God's own Son.

Just before taking them up that mountain, he had told them the reason for his going to Jerusalem, and he would tell them again of his suffering and death in Jerusalem. But, to give them strength, he would be transfigured before them, and they would see his glory, and hear the voice of his Father say: "This is my chosen Son; listen to him."

It seems strange that Jesus should be comforting THEM because of HIS pending suffering and death. Why are they (who have been told what is to come) not the ones to comfort Jesus? In fact, why is Jesus always the one to be the strong one, the comforter, the consoler? Why is there not someone to comfort and console him? After all, is not Jesus the One who is in need here and now? Let me digress a moment.

There's one in every family. I suspect that there is one in your family. There's one in any social grouping, whether a family or a close-knit group of friends. I am talking about the person that is the one to whom others turn in times of difficulty, or strife or death or any other tough situation. You know who I mean - the one who is expected to be cool, to know what to do, and then to do it, and do it right.

I don't know how it happens, but it does. It is something that just happens in nearly every family, or every community of friends. Someone is seen as the one to handle the difficult times, no matter whether they have the experience or ability, and no matter whether they want to be in that position. I see it every time I attend a dying, a crisis, or a death. There is one person in each family that is the "strong one," on whom the others depend for strength.

Being a parish priest, I am often put in such a position. "He's the pastor. He'll know what to do." "We can turn to him to give us the strength." "He will tell us what to do." "He will know what to say, and he will make it all right again."

Such are the expectations of the one that each family has designated, and such are the roles that a pastor is assigned. But there is a difficulty in this phenomenon for me. Yes, the pastor is the one with the training and experience to handle many crises, to comfort many in distress or difficulty. But, there are times when even the pastor is not in the position to be THE ONE who can make things all right, or even comfortable for others.

Let me give you an example so you understand what I mean. When I was a first-year seminarian, I was assigned to a parish in Radford for the summer. One of my happiest tasks there was to visit a family regularly whose son, aged 12, was in an accident that left him brain-stem damaged and paralyzed. Kevin was a delight, and required physical therapy twice daily, with three or four volunteers each time. That was a lot of volunteers to organize to help do Kevin's Physical Therapy. But we did it, and then told stories, laughed, and made Kevin laugh and know that one day he would again be able to speak, to walk and to be a regular guy. And Kevin believed that, just as we did. So, he endured the pain and stress of the twice-daily physical therapy to get back control of his muscles and speech.

I left Radford after three months and returned to seminary for the second year. I took with me so many fond memories, most especially of Kevin and his family. I was back at seminary for only a week when the call came that Kevin did not wake up that morning. All those many months of believing, all those many months of therapy, of laughter, of hopes for a future. It was all gone, and Kevin was dead.

I made plans to go to Radford, and was invited to give the eulogy at the funeral. I was in such deep pain, so sad, so in need of comfort and consolation. I couldn't wait to get back to Radford so that I might be consoled, loved, somehow made to believe that this tragedy was tolerable. So I arrived at Radford, seeking comfort in my mourning and sadness, hoping to find some solace in my pain. But when I arrived, there was no comfort to be found, because there was none to be offered, at least, not to me. You see, I was the aspiring priest, the parish's seminarian. At the wake service, at the house, and at the funeral, I was expected to be the giver of comfort and solace, the source of strength and hope. I was not to be the receiver of comfort. I was not allowed to be someone in need of mourning. No one would comfort me.

Who ministers to the minister? Who consoles the consoler? Who helps the helper? No one. No one. No one.

Still, there's one in every family. There's one in every social grouping. There is that person to whom others turn, with a strong and clear expectation that they will be the strong one, that they will know what to say, and that they will say it. Suddenly, at Kevin's funeral, I came to learn that, as a priest, I was always assumed to be that person. And that was ok most of the time, that is, at the times when the people who were the objects of the crisis were not personally involved in my life. But for the times when I too was someone in pain, grieving or sadness, there would still be the expectation that I would be the giver, and never the recipient of, the solace, comfort and pastoral care.

Who, I ask again, comforts the comforter? Who ministers to the minister? Who consoles the consoler?

The years have passed and I am a priest now, and have had many wonderful opportunities to provide pastoral care and the love of Christ to many in pain and suffering. That experience at Kevin's death has recurred many times, when I have had to mask or hide my own deep sadness or sorrow so that I could serve others. I am getting good at it. And, serving God's people is a great source of strength. Still, when it is all done, sometimes I go home and I cry by myself. I stress out. I ache in my heart and soul. And I wonder: Who will comfort the comforter? And who will minister to the minister?

We are all people. We often ignore the people in our lives who do the most for us, simply because we have come to expect of them the wondrous gifts they give us. We take for granted our parents who sacrifice and love us, who give to us until they have little for themselves. We take for granted our friends and co-workers who are there when we are blue, who bring us a gift, or a smile, or a hug, when we are hurting. We don't pay attention to them, because they are paying attention to us, and that is just what we want, and it is exactly what we expect them to do. But, don't you wonder yourself: Do they ever need an arm around their shoulder, a hug around the neck, a whispered word of confidence, an unearned smile?

Is there not someone that you owe an arm-around-the-shoulder, a hug-around-the-neck, a whispered word of confidence?

MEDITATIONS AFTER ORDINATION

With ordination as a Catholic priest, an intense time of personal reflection began. The wonder and awe of being able to serve the family of God as an ordained minister was so strong that it nearly overwhelmed me at first. There were feelings of unworthiness, intense gratitude, and awe-filled joy at who and what I had become. I felt unworthy to be a priest; I was not holy, not particularly spiritual, and maybe not a very good person. Still, here I was, a priest of God. So I felt amazing gratitude at becoming something and someone I had never imagined, someone I had not even considered to become, and someone who fought the possibility for several years. (Yes, the ideas of priesthood came to me while in prayer during those years of single parenthood, but I wanted to marry again, did not want to grow old alone.)

But mostly I felt awe, an awe that brought a joy that was sometimes giddy, and sometimes sublime. "So this was why God spoke to me on the Green Field of the American University of Beirut so many years ago!" "So this is what God was preparing me for!" Looking back in retrospection, it seemed naive that I never noticed it before, that all the many experiences, the education, and the life skills that were creating me as a particular person, were forming me to become a priest. Some people would ask me, as a newly-ordained priest of age 52 why I waited so long. I could honestly reply that it was not I who waited, but it was God who was waiting until he had formed me into the particular person that he needed to be a priest. And I believe that totally - I could not have been the priest that God was calling until, and unless, I had lived and grown to become this particular person and, now, priest.

Below are some of the early reflections on my life's journey, as a newly-ordained priest.

My Daily Prayer

18th Sunday, A: Isaiah 55:1-3, Matthew 14:13-21

It went by so fast that I'll bet you missed it. I'll have to admit I missed it the first time I read through the gospel. But this is what happened: Jesus blessed the bread, but Jesus did not distribute it himself.   Listen again to what I just read: *Taking the five loaves and the two fish, and looking up to heaven, he said the blessing, broke the loaves, and gave them to the disciples, who in turn gave them to the crowds.* (Matthew 14:19)

Nowhere in the gospel is the role of the disciple clearer than in this reading today. The story of the feeding of the five thousand tells us that Jesus gave the blessed bread and fish to the disciples and the disciples gave them to the crowd. Jesus worked through the hands of the disciples that day. And he still does today. That's the point.

Here we come face to face with the essential truth of being a Christian disciple of Jesus: It is true that the disciple is helpless without the Lord. But it is also true that the Lord is helpless without his disciples today. If Jesus wants something done today, if he wants a child taught, a sick person visited, or someone to be forgiven, he has to have a human person to do it. God needs people through whom to act, speak, and love. It is that simple. So, being a disciple, a believer, a Christian, means letting the Lord use you and all your gifts to do his work on earth.

My daily prayer, one which I say every morning, and then repeat every time I am called upon to serve someone is this: "Lord, here's my mind, my heart, my hands and my voice. I give them to you to do your work. And Lord, I will try to stay out of the way." Even when I was preparing to come to read the gospel and speak, I said that prayer. I can do and be nothing, and I don't want to try to be or do anything, except with and in the Lord. If something goes well, I thank the Lord for using me; and I don't try to take credit for it.

When Jesus was on the earth, he gave us only one prayer to say, Jesus told that, every time we pray to the Father, we are to say those words. One of the wonderful phrases in the prayer which Jesus taught is: "Thy kingdom come." What an incredible thing for Jesus to tell us to say! Why do we say

"Thy kingdom come"? Surely, God's kingdom will come, is coming, irrespective of whether we pray for it to come or not. Or - will it??

Is the kingdom of God, which Jesus announced and began, here now and continuing to come in its fullness? Do we have a role, even a responsibility, in its unfolding? Or will it come no matter what, because God wills it? If we do not have a role, if it's going to come anyway, then why did Jesus tell us to pray "Thy kingdom come" to the Father every time we pray?

The implication of Jesus telling us to say this is that we do play a role in the coming of God's kingdom, that we do participate in its unfolding, or that we can forestall it, or even stop its coming if we want. And that is quite true!

Our God, who in his great love created us, gave us free will (freedom), and we can choose to do his will or not. We can choose to participate in the unfolding of his eternal communion, or ignore it, or even work against it. And because of this loving gift of freedom, and because God wants us to choose to use our freedom in bringing his kingdom to fullness, Jesus asks us all to pray "Thy kingdom come."

When we say "Thy kingdom come," we are saying to God: "May your kingdom come in me, through me, to others, to all creation." We are offering ourselves as instruments of the unfolding of the kingdom. We are agreeing to participate in the work of bringing the kingdom to its fullness. So we need to be careful what we pray for - Do we really mean it and want God to use us as instruments of his love?

Jesus Christ needs people through whom he can work and through whom his truth and his love can enter into the lives of others. He needs men and women to whom he can give, in order that they may give to others. Without such people, God cannot get the work of building his kingdom done.

It may seem like an impossible task and we could become discouraged by such an assignment. But, in this gospel story of the feeding of the five thousand, there is something else to give us comfort. At the beginning, when Jesus told his disciples to feed the crowd, they told Jesus that they only had five loaves and two fish; yet, with that paltry sum which they brought to him, Jesus worked a miracle. Jesus sets every one of us the tremendous task of communicating himself to others; but he does not demand from us greatness in skill and heart that we do not have. Jesus says to us: "Come to me as you are, however ill-equipped. Bring to me what you have and are, however little. And I will use it greatly in the service of the kingdom." Little, even very little (such as five barley loaves and two fish) is always great and mighty in the hands of the Lord.

A final thought: How would you feel about entrusting your new car in the hands of a 16-year-old new driver? Or how would you feel if the one investing your money, maybe all your retirement funds, was an uneducated person who knew very little about finances, economics, or planning? Of course, you'd feel terrible, and you simply wouldn't let incompetent and unskilled people do work for you. No one would take such a risk of having someone mishandle their valuable things.

But consider Jesus' position. He was sent to earth to teach all how to live and love in the kingdom of God. He brought that kingdom to earth, but he did not complete it. There was never a more important task than the one of Jesus, a task given him by the Father. Yet, Jesus left this world with the work of building the kingdom incomplete. And, in his great love for us who call ourselves Christians, Jesus entrusted his work, the very work given him by the Father. Can you imagine such faith in us humans as to trust us with the most important task in human history??!! Yet, Jesus did do that. Jesus loves you and trusts you so much; Jesus has such complete faith in you that he actually believes that you will accept his offer to work for the kingdom, and do what he asked.

And you, you won't entrust a car or a pension to some naive amateur! Yet our God has entrusted the work of his kingdom to his disciples. And that means YOU - an amateur, a struggling Christian! What a faith Jesus has in you! Would that your faith may be even a hundredth time as strong.

(Bow and pray to God): Lord, make us instruments of your peace. Replace out selfish desires and needs and wants, with a love for you and a desire to do your will. Choose us as you chose the disciples, use us with God as our source for your power and action in the world, and send us, Lord, to the nations to proclaim your kingdom, by our words, by our actions, by our living and our dying.

Our Father in heaven, may your kingdom come, in us, through us, for others.

Zechariah's Silence

4th Sunday of Advent, C: Micah 5:1-4a, Hebrews 10:5-10, Luke 1:39-45

[This homily came out of a reflection on my daily prayer and the homily above. It shows my realization that I must make my prayer a public prayer, not just a personal and quiet prayer.]

He was really worried about his wife. She was confused, she was scared, she was old, and she was pregnant. She was wondering if all the world had gone crazy. Ever since he came home from the Temple a few months ago, he couldn't speak. She did not know why. And he couldn't tell her that their about-to-be-born baby was a special gift from God, and that an angel told him so.

If she could read, he would write for her what had happened - to him, to her, and to them. He'd tried some sign language but ... how do you tell your wife that an angel appeared to you and said that, although elderly and childless, you were going to have a baby? Trying to "sign" to her only frightened and confused her more.

Now she sat and prayed and got bigger with child, and sat and prayed some more. She couldn't go outside because she was laughed at by the younger women who were amazed to see her in this condition. So she asked God for understanding. Actually, she probably pleaded for understanding.

How Zachariah wished God would answer her prayer, maybe send an angel to her. She needed God and now!

Sometimes when things seem out of control, it is hard to believe that God is working in our lives, giving us experiences that don't seem like gifts of love. But when we look back, as Elizabeth would one day do, we can see the wonderful effect of God's loving plan in our lives. God does have a plan and we are part of it.

But, back to the story. Next there was a commotion out front of their house. Zachariah went out, only to discover Elizabeth's teenage cousin arriving for an unexpected visit. What a scene - a mute old man and a journey-weary traveler! Mary had walked for three or four days into the hill country. You can just imagine how Mary looked, and smelled, after such a trip.

Zachariah shuffled himself and Mary into the house. He had hardly gotten to Elizabeth (who was keeping out of sight) when an amazing thing happened. As if he had not seen enough, been overwhelmed enough by the angel's visit, now the most incredible thing happened.

Elizabeth forgot herself and her fears. She looked at her little cousin like God himself had come in answer to her prayers. And she said: "Who am I that the mother of my Lord should come to me?" And, to verify the presence of the Lord, even the baby in her womb leaped for joy. Elizabeth knew. She knew. Suddenly it all made sense to her, and God had answered her prayers with a personal visit. She would never be the same again. God came to her. God came into the world and she, Elizabeth, recognized his presence.

God answered her prayers when she needed it most. God was there for her; the Spirit of God filled her and she was given understanding. The very moment the Lord was in her presence, she knew for certain. Without a hesitation or a doubt.

But maybe we don't agree. Maybe we are thinking that we would recognize the Lord in our midst if he showed up. Maybe we do not think Elizabeth or her baby so special in this regard. Well, consider this: The Lord Jesus whom Mary brought into Elizabeth's presence is the same Lord that each of us has brought here today in our hearts. So turn and stare at someone; I mean it, turn and stare. And consider the possibility that you are looking at a modern version of Mary who has brought Christ's presence here today.

But let's finish the story. What about Zachariah? What is he feeling? I'd guess he was also leaping for joy as his baby did, that he was so awed by the recognition of God's presence. Imagine his utter pain at not being able to speak, not being able to welcome the Lord. If he could only talk, he'd have something to say. He would praise God and thank God and tell God of his love and trust, and then he would praise and thank some more. If only he could talk!

If Jesus came into our midst, we'd have something to say. *[a declaration with certainty.]* We'd not keep silent, would we? *[again, with doubt, questioning]* We wouldn't, would we??? *(Pause)* Would we???

My Wooden Chalice

Christmas Mass at Midnight: Isaiah 9:1-6, Titus 2:11-14, Luke 2:1-14

Christmas is about a Father's love. It is all about a Father who has loved his children so very much. From the very beginning of time.

Now, at Christmas we celebrate with praise and thanksgiving to Our Father the greatest gift of His love - the gift of His Son Incarnate - here and now, as a testament of His love, as a witness for our love, and in anticipation of being united with Love Itself at the end of time.

Tonight/today I would like the opportunity to preach especially to the children who are here. So, at this time, I invite all the children to listen carefully as I reflect on our readings.

Today we celebrate the birth of Christ, the feast of Christmas, and I am so happy and excited. See how I am dressed in white? This garment is called a "chasuble" and this is a "stole"; they were made for me by my mother. You may think it a simple thing for my mother to do - make this chasuble and stole - but it wasn't. She has a disease called rheumatoid arthritis, and her hands are painful and misshapen due to the disease. It must have been very painful and difficult for her to make this for me to wear when I celebrate Mass. Why do you suppose she endured all that pain just to make me this white chasuble and stole?

I'll tell you why. She loves me. And, because she loves me, she is willing to suffer pain in order to bring me joy. She is like Jesus. Jesus suffered very much. Our gospel stories tell us that Jesus gave his whole life for love of us - so that his joy may be ours and our joy may be complete. That is what our parents do for us. Today as we hear how God, like a parent, offers himself to us through his Son Jesus in order to teach us about how we can love others. It is good to pause and recall that the love which Jesus gives to us came, first of all, from our parents.

I am very happy today. I can feel Jesus' love for me through the love of my parents. And I can pass on the love that Jesus has for me, to others, because my parents gave me the gift of love. And God gave that love to them first of all, through the birth of Jesus into the world.

Jesus says so often that we should love each other: *"This is the commandment we have from him: whoever loves God must also love his brother."* (1 John 4:21) The way that we can feel the love of Jesus is to feel the love of others. The way that we can share Jesus' love is to give our love to others. You see, Jesus says that he is with us always, and that he will remain with us always. But how can that be? We can't see him right now; we can't touch; we can't hear him. But we can see, touch, and hear each other. And that is where we can find Jesus - in each other. We can feel Jesus' love when we feel others' love. Just like my mother's love for me is really Jesus' love for me.

That is the point. God is love. When we love others, we make God more present in our lives, and to others. So love one another. Make Jesus more present in the world. Let others love you too.

If we all got together and decided to forgive everyone, and to love everyone, I wonder if we could actually see Jesus among us? I think so.

Now let me speak to the parents, guardians, family and friends of these children. You are the ones through whom these children first experience the love of Jesus. By your actions and words, you communicate whatever understanding of love these children know. In simple words, you are the instruments of making God, a God who is love, present to these children. It is an awesome responsibility.

If a child grows without love, or with a misshapen or conditional sense of love, that child is being denied access to the experience of God. For the scripture says: *everyone who loves is begotten by God and knows God. Whoever is without love does not know God.* (1 John:7-8) Do not let these children be without love. Show them love; show them God.

It may sound corny and simple. If so, then Jesus' teaching is corny and simple. But that's ok. "God is love." It is that simple. If you want to make God visible in your life, in your family, in the world, love (and that includes forgiving), and let others love you. Christmas is the birth of Perfect Love in our world.

Now let me tell you another story about the love of the Father. On my first birthday, I moved into the home where my parents still live. My Dad built it himself. You see, like Jesus Christ, my Dad was a carpenter. He built that home more than fifty years ago, and later made much of the furniture in it too. When I was a kid, my Dad was not around much, because a carpenter is at the beck and call of other people's needs, the weather, and the work. I resented it that Dad was not able to be home more. As I grew, I dreamed of the day when he might invite me to come into the woodshop and work with him. Making something together would be the most wonderful proof of our love, I felt. Then it happened. When my older brother Joe and I were in junior high school, Dad got some old bowling pins at the Catholic Young Men's Association club, made of hard maple wood, and told us he would show us how to use the lathe. With Dad's help (he did about 40% of the work, and I did about 60%), we made a small cup, rather like a fat chalice. I rubbed it with linseed oil, and cared for it so much. It symbolized the love of my father for me, and I treasured our time together. As I grew, I took that cup to college and used it as a pencil holder. When I got married and had kids, it was where I put the loose change from my pockets - my kids got their change and lunch money from that cup. Finally, after the kids were grown and I entered seminary, I took that cup - symbol of parental love - with me and kept it on the shelf of my room.

As I got closer to ordination I decided I wanted that symbol of my father's love to be my chalice. I searched until I found a chalice maker in Canada who said they could drill a hole down through it, fit in a golden cup, and add a gold base too. Here is it with me today - the work of a father and his son, from about 40+ years ago, the proof of a father's love, a love that also gave me my faith, my Catholic religion, and that empowered me to share the same with my children, and now with you this Christmas night/day.

Today as I offer that cup of wine to my heavenly Father, I will thank God for the gift of his love, for his presence to me, given first of all to me through the love of my parents. The cup is engraved on the bottom: "From my father's hands into my Father's hands." Each time I raise that cup of the new covenant, I will praise God for being love, for being my parents' love, and for choosing me to offer my father's cup as my Father's cup of salvation.

Yes, God is love, and God wants us to share him with others. He gives us the experience of his love, first of all, in parents. It is that love of God which our faith calls us to give.

Living is about loving. The experience of love is the experience of

Christ coming anew into our hearts and lives. Loving makes Christmas come true every time.

Be like my Dad.   Be like my Mom. Be like Jesus: Love one another, even if it hurts sometimes.

Dad Fell Again.

16th Sunday, C: Genesis 18:1-10a, Luke 10:38-42

In January 1998, Dad fell three times and, each time, broke a bone. When he had the casts on and could do very little, he became so depressed. He is a father and grandfather, a husband, an electrician and carpenter, a farmer, and he could not DO anything relative to these self-designations. Like so many of us, Dad defines himself, and maybe his worth, in terms of what he does. He forgets that he is a creation of God, one who is loved just as he is, and not for what he can do or accomplish.

So often we forget that God loves us just as we are, and that we do not have to do anything to earn his love - that, no matter what condition is our lives, we can be the very person God wants us to be. It is not what we do, but who we are, that matters; not what we do, but why we do it that defines us.

Today's readings can shed some light on God's love for us and his expectations of us. Our readings offer two famous biblical scenes of hospitality -- Abraham receiving the three travelers, and Martha and Mary hosting Jesus.

In the first reading, Abraham displays exacting desert hospitality to three men and, even before he realizes that one is God, he offers them precious water and food, and washes their feet. In so doing, Sarah and the servants comply with custom and stay in the background, doing the work. It is noteworthy that Abraham and Sarah obey all the cultural expectations of the day for hospitality and behavior.

In the gospel we see that Jesus does not follow the cultural expectations of his time, but enters the home of unmarried women, treats them with respect, speaking and acting directly with them. Jesus does not let these things get in the way of his sharing his good news of love and repentance and hope. The sister Mary seems to overcome behavioral and cultural expectations too, for she sits at Jesus' feet and listens; she does not enter into the social prescriptions of cleaning the house, preparing food and directing servants. Her priority is the Lord's message.

In contrast, Martha is obedient to the expectations of a good Jewish hostess toward a guest. She becomes very involved in doing the preparations.

Her priority is to do what is expected, even though "the Lord" is present. When she asks the Lord to tell her sister to get involved in the preparations, he is quick to reply. Mary has chosen the better part and she is not to be denied. That is, Mary has recognized that this is an occasion to get beyond social expectations (There will be plenty of time for that!) and she concentrates on God's presence of himself as gift. After all, Jesus did not come to receive a service but to present a gift!

Martha, however, cannot stop doing what she feels necessary to serve her guest. She is like so many of us who feel that we must do something to please the Lord. But the Lord does not ask for anything but that we accept the gift of his word and, with its reception, let it guide our actions.

Jesus is not saying that it is better to sit and pray than it is to serve the Lord. That is clearly not what the gospel writer Luke had in mind since this story follows directly after the story of the Good Samaritan as a model of how we love our neighbor. It is not what we do but why we do it that matters.

Martha is ... *anxious and upset about many things....* (Luke 10:41) Her focus is on the activities of welcoming her guest, not on the guest himself. When Jesus says Mary has chosen the better portion, it is that Mary has chosen to make Jesus alone her focus. Martha has let her preparations become her focus.

Again, Martha is like many of us. She has let her goal become the doing of her hospitality tasks, forgetting for a moment that they are not ends in themselves, but are the means to welcoming the Lord. Perhaps she is like us parents who become so obsessed with our jobs so that we forget that the purpose of our work is meeting the needs of the family, and the needs of the family include love and quality time together away from work. Or perhaps Martha is like the Christians who become so focused on ritual and prescription in prayer that they forget that their real end and goal is the love and praise of God.

"Martha, Martha, you are anxious and upset about so many things." (Luke 10:41) But I have come to offer you something, and you need to do nothing. I love you just as you are and want nothing but your reception of my gift. Martha, Martha, you are exactly who and what I love and desire to gift. Nothing is required of you.

And that brings me back to Dad who is once again hospitalized and feeling depressed because he cannot do anything. "Dad, Dad, you are anxious and upset about so many things. But even in your sickness and disability, you are the very person God loves and has come to as 'gift.'" By your very being, you can allow God to become present to others. In your limitations, you can allow God to make his message of love become real. Let others love you and serve you, and pray for you, that they might experience God's love, the power of prayer, and God's gift of healing. Let God use you just as you are -- be an instrument for the spreading of the gospel of love."

No matter what is our condition or state, *"There is need for only one thing,"* (Luke 10:42) Jesus says -- to accept the gift of God's word in our lives' to let God use us to make his love apparent in the world.

I Never Saw My Father Cry Before.

6th Sunday of Easter, B: 1 John 4:7-10, John 15:9-17

Our readings today are full of risk-taking love. Jesus loves all his children with an uncompromising love that shows deep faith in his followers, with great hopes that they would *go and bear fruit that will remain.* (John 15:16) This kind of love which Jesus gives us is nearly impossible to imagine. I suppose the closest thing we might imagine is the deep love our parents show to us when they receive children in their lives, develop hopes for them, and then have faith in all that they are and might be.

My Dad had hopes. All parents do. Let me tell you a story and maybe you'll understand how important it is to hope, to be hoped for, and to have your hopes be realized.

I'd never seen my dad cry before. But through his tears, I heard him tell me how being a parent was a big gamble; how he'd invested many years raising us kids, an investment with no guarantees of a return. But as he sat there in his new wheelchair and crying tears of joy, I realized how grateful Dad was to know that his children had become everything that he had hoped they would be. While he spent that summer near death in three hospitals, his five children rallied around him and Mom, to stay around the clock at his bedside, to take care of the house, the chores, and the finances, and to love and support each other. Now Dad was back home, alive, and, in remembering all that had happened that summer, he got to see his big gamble of hopes and faith and love pay off! That's what he was crying about with joy that August a couple of years ago.

Everyone has hopes and dreams for the future.
- We hope for our families, our children, ourselves.
- Our prayers reflect our hopes for ourselves and others.

Dad had hopes for his kids and so he prayed for them.

But, to hope is to have faith. For without faith, there is no hope. Faith is the basis of all hope.
- Only if we believe that something is possible can we then hope for it to be.
- Only if we believe in others can we have hope in them.

Dad believed in his kids, and in his ability to teach them.

It is love for others that gives us faith in them.

- We can believe in those we love.

- We can believe in those who love us.

It's love that grounds faith in others. Like Dad's love for his kids.

But loving others is a risk. The more we love, the more we take risks.

- We risk that our love will not be returned;

- We risk that our faith in those we love will be in vain;

- We risk that the ones we believe in will not fulfill our hopes for them.

Loving is risky business; and lovers are gamblers.

Parents know all about the risks of hoping, of having faith, and of loving. They gamble in their love for each child. When a child is born, there is an immediate sense of love for the new one, no matter how many others, no matter the circumstances. This parental love causes one to do things that one would do for no one but a child. All the while, the parent shares, gives, loves, has faith in, and hopes for the child. But there is the sure knowledge that it is a big risk - that this child might not love back, might disappoint, might not fulfill hopes and dreams. But still, the parent plods on diligently and patiently, investing love, and faith and hope. Like my Dad did all those years of parenting! Because that is what a parent does. A parent hopes, a parent loves, simply loves, and trusts and hopes.

Jesus took risks too! And Jesus had hopes. His hopes were that his disciples would believe in him and that his work would be continued after he was gone. He showed himself to his disciples, and expressed his deep love and confidence in them. We heard it in our gospel reading.

And he trusted that his hopes would be fulfilled, because he had faith in those to whom he entrusted the work. He must have truly believed in the disciples in order to entrust them with his own work, the work that His Father had given Him to do. He hoped that those he taught would show the same deep faith in him.

To have such faith in others required love, deep love. A love like that would have to be like the love which Jesus shared with His Father. And it was; that is exactly what it was. We heard in the second reading: *As the Father loves me, so I also love you.* (John 15:9) That is why Jesus could have such a faith in others; because He gave them the task of continuing his work and, in so doing, he gave them the very love of himself and his Father.

Even more than that, so that they would be sure to accept His love, and live up to the faith he had in them to fulfill his hopes, He made them promises: He promised to be with them always; to be in them while they were continuing his work, and then, when they were done with His work, He promised to bring them to spend eternity with him in heaven.

Now, I said earlier that to hope and love is a risk. It sure seems that Jesus was a risk-taker. I guess you could say that Jesus was a gambler. At least that is what I would call a guy who would put all his eggs in one basket:

- A guy who would spend his life spreading his Father's message and then, just as he is about to die, entrust all his work to a small band of amateurs whom he hoped had believed his message.
- A guy who would give up his life, with a confidence that others would continue the work: to do what he did - just because he loved them. To continue his mission, to keep his work alive. Even knowing that doing this work meant suffering and maybe death. Yes, that Jesus must have been a gambler!

He must have loved them very much though, as much as He and His Father loved each other.

But how could he believe, how could he trust that they loved him just as much as He loved them? After all, the apostles certainly showed limited faith in the gospels. Boy, that Jesus was a gambler!

And, what if the disciples were just as he hoped? And did what he asked of them? What if they did tell others the message that he preached, about his Father and the love he offered? Still: How could Jesus hope and trust that the ones they would tell about Jesus would continue to pass it on? How could Jesus be so naive as to think that you can trust people generation after generation down to today? That Jesus was quite a gambler.

Where did Jesus ever think He would find people who cared that much about Him, and His Father's work, and His Love and His promises? Who'd ever bet on a gambler like Jesus?

I would. I will! In fact, I'll bet my life. Because I would give anything if someday I could see Jesus cry tears of joy over me just like my Dad did that August.

Picking Up Coins

16th Sunday, B: Mark 6:30-34

It all started out as a game between my father and me. We both had bad eyes, especially problems with depth perception. So, because of that, we always walked with our eyes looking down on the ground in front of us so that we would not stumble. A silly consequence of our looking at the ground instead of straight ahead was that we saw many things that most people would not see. In particular we found lots of coins. Mostly pennies and sometimes dimes, more rarely a nickel or a quarter. Dad started to pick them up and he would announce periodically how much he had found. As a result, I started to do it too, because I too saw many as I watched the ground as I walked. Pretty soon it was a sort of competition to see who found the most money or the most coins.

Eventually it grew to be more than a game. It became humiliating for me. I still picked up the coins I found, but it was hard to do so in public. It was embarrassing to pick up a penny if someone was watching. In my egotistic way, I was afraid of what people would think of me. "Is he so poor, or so tight, that he needs every penny he sees?" they might be thinking. Some people even kidded me if they saw me pick up a coin. That was how it became an act of humility. Even if people were looking, I would pick up a coin I found, and then remind myself of the importance of humility, of not worrying about what others thought of me, and of letting other people think what they would.

After some time, a new realization came to me, and my picking up coins took on a whole new meaning, one that has enriched my prayer life and my spirituality tremendously. When I saw a coin on the ground as I was out for a walk or a run, I'd bend over and pick it up. Then I'd say a prayer of thanksgiving to God for this free gift that he has given to me. I'd recall with gratitude that all that I have and all that I am has been given to me freely by a God who loves me. So I was saying a prayer of thanksgiving to God for his goodness to me. Now, every time I pick up a coin, it is an occasion to pray in thanksgiving to God.

If I tell you that I find about fifty cents a month that means that I say a prayer of thanksgiving, remembering how dependent I am on God's goodness, between 10 and 25 times a month. And, as I say these prayers, I reflect on particular things God has given me in my life. And it causes me to marvel at God's wonderful bounty. More than that, it reminds me to take care of, and use properly all that God has given me. For to ignore the gifts I have been given, or to use them improperly, is to be ungrateful for all I have and am. Which brings me to our gospel today.

In the gospel, the apostles return to Jesus, after going out and doing all that he had told them to do. They were tired, very tired, but willing to do more. Jesus' response to their return is quite remarkable. He said to them: *"Come away by yourselves to a deserted place and rest a while."* (Mark 6:31) Jesus noticed their tiredness; Jesus saw that they did not even have a chance to eat. So Jesus told them to go and take care of themselves. Jesus wanted them to take care of the most important thing the Father had given to them - their very selves.

The apostles, like so many of us, can become workaholics, ignoring our bodies, our health, our very selves. We may justify it by saying that we are sacrificing ourselves for others: our children, an aging parent, a growing family, or some other justification. But the truth of the matter is that we are not taking care of ourselves, not valuing the gift of ourselves that God has given to us when we ignore our own selves.

Who is not familiar with the story of the seven days of creation in Genesis? It ends with the wonderful verse: *Since on the seventh day God was finished with the work he had been doing, he rested on the seventh day from all the work he had undertaken* (Genesis 2:2).

It can occur in so many ways too, not just workaholism. There is the spouse who stays in an abusive marriage for years, saying that it is for the good of the kids when in reality, the children are suffering in the environment just as much as the parents. There is the person who leaves for work before the family is up and returns after they are back in bed, saying that the extra pay will be for the good of the family. But, what family is there when a parent is mostly absent.

Jesus is compared to a good shepherd in the end of our gospel passage today. He sees people in need, and *his heart was moved with pity for them, it says.* (Mark 6:34) That is our God, our loving savior. He cares for us, he sees us in our needs, and he wants to help us. Why? Because he loves us deeply, as he loves all that God has created. And if Jesus loves us so very much, then we too must love ourselves as well. That means we must take care of ourselves, with the same love and tenderness that Jesus has for each of us.

We are living in a society and a time when our self worth is often defined by what we can do, and how much we can accomplish, rather than by who and what we are (children of God, loved by God, and created for his Kingdom). It is easy to get caught up in the false acceptance that we are what we do, and then to try to do more than is necessary for our daily living.

If you are one of those who is not taking care of yourself, not respecting the most wonderful gift that God has given you - your very self - then may this Mass be the occasion when you hear Jesus say to you: *"Come away by yourselves to a deserted place and rest a while."* (Mark 6:31)

And as you rest, may you find many pennies of gratitude in your journey through life.

MEDITATIONS ON PRIESTHOOD

In this final section, I have included some homilies about life as a parish priest, albeit a unique parish priest by some traditional standards.

There is little to say about these homilies, as there is little to say about my formative years as a priest. There is much joy, but there is sadness; there is much life, but there is also death. The life of a parish priest brings the fullness of living and dying into daily reality. In doing so, it brings the meaning of the gospel of Jesus Christ into daily reality too.

Living is about dying to this life in order to be born anew to eternal life. In our baptisms we begin a journey whose goal is to die so as to rise with Christ. As a parish priest, I am humbly blessed to share in many people's journeys from that birth to that re-birth.

There is not much more to say than that. Except to say Thank You, God, for choosing me and for using me.

As I said for the first time so long ago, hiding with a blind man under some stone stairs at American University of Beirut, my daily prayer: "Lord, here is my heart, my hands, my voice and my mind. I give them to you to do your work. And I'll try to stay out of the way."

Playing "Twenty Questions"

2nd Sunday, C: Isaiah 62:1-5, 1 Corinthians 12:4-11, John 2:1-11

When I came here to Saint Edward Church, I knew some of the people in the parish. Others I thought I recognized, but could not place. One particular man fascinated me, because I was sure I knew him but couldn't identify how we were connected to each other. For some of the people I met here, I recognized them immediately and could say how we knew each other. For some, we were on Curcillo together, for others we worked together at the Medical College of Virginia (MCV). Two did their masters degrees under my supervision. Another used to go to my former parish of St. Ann's in Ashland, and some others knew me from St. Benedict Church where I was a deacon. It was easy to identify them. But then there was this guy Jerry whom I was sure I knew, but I couldn't figure it out. We played "Twenty Questions" but could not find the connection - he did not work with me at MCV; his children were a different age; we didn't go to the same gym or grocery store or pharmacy. He was younger, from a different area, and there seemed no connection between us. At least there was just no connection we could figure out. Jerry was sure that we did not know each other.

As the months moved on, we played "Twenty Questions" each time we met, for I was sure we knew each other. Finally after four months, it came to me who he was -- When he got out of college, his first job was in the same building where I worked. He passed me every day at The James Center, although we didn't work together. His was just a face I said "hello" to every day for several years, back in the late eighties.

In telling you this story, I wanted to share with you my belief that, if we work at it hard enough, we can find ourselves related to nearly anyone in some fashion. The world of humanity is interconnected; we are not strangers to others, even if we seem to think we are. God has intended that we be mutually inter-dependent and supportive of each other. To assure this, God has given each of us different gifts - strengths, weaknesses, life experiences, backgrounds - creating much diversity out of which comes a collage of humanity -- people connected to each other by their need to love, support and respect each other. That is exactly the point which Saint Paul was addressing in the letter to the Corinthians today.

This beautiful passage from Paul on the gifts of the Spirit is a celebration of what it means to live in a Christian community. Despite great diversity and different outlooks, there is one Spirit, who inspires all activity for the sake of the common good. Our challenge is to recognize both our own gifts and those of other members of our communities, in order to build up the entire community as lovingly and effectively as possible. We need each other. No one can boast of his or her strengths or gifts either; they are all from God; and they are not for our own personal use but for the building up of the kingdom of God.

Some people have gifts which they don't even recognize. For some, their gifts are their very presence in the community; that is, they are people God sends into a community to be the means for others being able to share. For instance, some people have the gift of poverty, so that others who don't have this gift may have someone to love and support and distribute their gifts to. Some people have the gift of sadness, so that others who have the gift of joy may be able to share. Imagine a community where no one needed joy; what would you do with your ability to give joy?! Imagine having an excess of anything and there being no one to need it, or with whom you could share it.

Saint Paul continually needed to reprimand the members of the Corinthian community and guide them in their faith development. It wasn't that the Corinthians were faithless or wayward. Often the problem was precisely one of excessive enthusiasm. In worship, some were given spectacular signs of God's power in their lives, such as speaking in foreign tongues or prophesying God's messages. Paul reminded them that these are gifts from God and should not be sources of personal pride. Still others manifested God in their activities, even if their gifts were more subdued. Paul asserted that God, the source of all gifts, is One. There is one Spirit, one Lord (Jesus), one God. And the gifts given by the Spirit are given for the good of all.

It's in the very act of giving our gifts to others and in receiving those gifts from others that we build up the body of Christ on earth. It is precisely in the giving and receiving of Love that we make Christ a real presence in our lives and in our community. We hear it in the scriptures over and over again: *God is love and he who lives in love lives in God, and God lives in him.* It is the giving and receiving of our gifts - the giving and receiving of Love; the giving and receiving of God who is Love - that we become the Body of Christ, that is, the Body of God, that is, the Body of Love.

God gives us his love, so that we might give it to others and, thereby, make his presence more a reality in the world. So we can't brag of our gifts! We can't withhold our gifts! We can't feel better or worse than anyone else about the gifts we have. We are all one; we all have different gifts, but they are for the mutual benefit of all.

Before you criticize anyone, consider that that person is somehow connected to you, related to you in the Body of Christ. You need them and they need you, even if you do not know how or why - such as I could not figure out how and why I knew Jerry here at St. Edward's.

- Before you criticize the woman who had an abortion this week, look around you; she is sitting right behind you and needs your prayers and love, not your condemnation.

- Before you say that the man in jail ought to be executed, consider his kids; they go to school with yours and they need support and love, not anger and revenge.

- Before you look at that terminally ill old lady and say she ought to die, consider her son who works with you; he has not yet told his mother he loves her, and she is waiting for that.

- Before you judge anyone, stop and consider the many ways they are related to you and those about you. We are in this journey of life together; we are all seeking the same goal - heaven. And, whether you want to accept it or not, our God loves everyone the same, and wants everyone to return to be together for all eternity. Our earthly inter-dependence is intended by God to last for all eternity.

This month we are focusing our human concerns on Respect for Life issues. When you show respect for the lives of others, you are showing respect for the Body of Christ - the one connected unity of which you are an integral part. Today as you leave Church, stop by the table in the Commons and learn how you can respect human life - all human life - by your own actions.

Now, look about you and ask yourself in amazement: Which of these people does God need for me to support? Which of these people will one day be my source of support and solace? May you find and give love throughout the entire body of Christ as you continue to grow toward your eternal destiny.

Sometimes I Am Scared Too.

8th Sunday, C: Sirach 27:4-7, Luke 6:39-45

The gospel really upset me when first I read it. *"Can a blind person guide a blind person? Will not both fall in a pit?"* (Luke 6:39) That phrase is the thing that upsets me, and scares me too. I'm a priest, and so many people expect me to help them, to be a light to guide them in their darkness. When I stand up here to preach, some people actually listen, and they want to hear God's words in their lives. And they expect me to guide them in this. But they only hear me, Chuck Breindel, a simple human person. It scares me.

Sometimes I feel like a blind person myself, struggling to get out of the blindness. No wonder those words scare me. No wonder I get upset at this gospel. I am not the One people need and want. I'm not the Light in the darkness. Sometimes I wonder if you all see and hear the very fragile and human guy who stands here before you each week. As Jeremiah said in our first reading: "When a sieve is shaken, the husks appear; so do one's faults when one speaks."

So why do I come back each week and get up here and try to say and do whatever I can so that you may have an experience of God's word in our lives? It is because I love you. And, in my naivety, I truly believe that God is love, and if I love, I am making God (who is Love) more visibly present for you. How very much I want you to feel the love I have for you! How much I want you to accept it, and pass it on to someone else! I wish I had some magic so I could cause you to love too. But I do not.

Or, maybe I do.

And maybe you do too! I have the courage to stand here, only because I firmly believe it is not I, Chuck Breindel, who is speaking, but Christ himself, who has accepted my offer to use me to speak to you. I can do this because I do not believe it is I, but Christ who lives in me, that is in control. I can do this because I've offered God the use of my voice, and mind and heart and hands, so he has someone to do his will here [at the parish]. And I believe God accepts anyone who is able to make such an offer of his or her life.

Sometimes people ask me if I get scared when I have to get up here in front of all of you. These people know me personally, and know of my shyness and insecurity. But I'm not scared at all. If I thought it were up to me to know what to say and how to speak, then I would be frightened to speak. But I don't have to worry about that - all I have to do is offer myself to God and then let him use me - and try to stay out of his way. So, in reality, it is not the blind leading the blind, when I get up here. It is God, and not me, and it is you, and not the blind. For you are not blind either, since the Spirit of God is in you too, by virtue of your baptisms.

In case you've not noticed it, nothing that I've said about myself depends on my being a priest. You too have the same ability - maybe a much greater ability - than I do to spread the "good news" of Jesus Christ to the world. I wonder if you are as scared as I could be at the possibility of letting God use you for his work in the world?

Are you scared to do God's work? Is your fear of letting others see and hear Christ in you the source of your fear? Does it keep you from reaching out to others, of speaking out when you see injustice or evil? If so, today is the day to change!! What have you got to lose?

I know the answer to that very question. What you have to lose is your family's or friends' good opinion of you. Why, if you start letting people recognize the presence of Christ in their lives, simply by your presence, your words and actions, you are scared that people will not like you, and may even mock you, laugh at you, or shun you. What is it you've got to lose? - Your sense of yourself that depends on others' liking you.

OK, perhaps that is too harsh. Maybe you too are feeling like "the blind leading the blind." Maybe you feel ill-equipped to be an instrument of God's love in the world, for your family and friends and coworkers.

Well, guess what? You're wrong. By your Baptism and Confirmation, you've received the gift of the Holy Spirit in you, and that Spirit will guide and direct, and use you to do God's work - If you will just give up your ego, your self-control, and be open to let Our Lord work in and through you. You'll discover, as I have, the incredible, almost unbelievable, experience of having God work through your mind and heart and voice.

You are a good person and, as Jesus says in our gospel, *A good person out of the store of goodness in his heart produces good ....* (Luke 6:45) You are a good person, you are a baptized Christian, you are a tabernacle of Christ and his Spirit.

What are you waiting for? When you leave here with an experience of his love and grace today, you are super-charged to be Christ for someone. Only you know who that someone is, and maybe you do not even know who will experience Christ in and through you. So, what are you waiting for? You are not blind either.

Traveling One-by-One, Not Two-by-Two

15th Sunday, B: Amos 7:12-15, Ephesians 1:3-14, Mark 6:7-13

Every three years when this particular gospel from Mark comes around, I feel a twinge of envy for those twelve apostles that Jesus sent out to help in the work of the Kingdom of God. If you heard that first line of the gospel, it says that *Jesus summoned the Twelve and began to send them out two by two....* (Mark 6:7) Those first ministers of Jesus did not work alone but had someone with them to help them, to share the burden, to support and care for them. That is the basis of my small twinge of envy - that they had a partner and did not work alone as ministers. How I wish that were possible today! But it is not possible in most of the world, because the number of priests is far too few to have them be sent out two by two. Instead the norm is to be alone as a priest, often serving more than one parish. In the western part of Virginia, there are many of our priests who serve two or three churches, for instance. On a weekend, they ride from church to church to celebrate Mass and the sacraments.

However, although I am the only priest here, or anywhere nearby, for that matter, I am not alone. For all of you are with me. And by the grace of your baptisms, you share in the priesthood of Jesus Christ. It is written this way in *The Dogmatic Constitution of the Church* (Chapter II: The People of God, 10): "Though they differ essentially and not only in degree, the common priesthood of the faithful and the ministerial or hierarchical priesthood are none the less ordered one to another; each in its own proper way shares in the one priesthood of Christ."

While the bishops now send out priests one by one, and not two by two, still the Holy Spirit works to bring a shared ministry between peoples - some of whom are ordained priests or deacons, and others lay people. They work cooperatively together to bring the work of Jesus to fullness on earth.

I guess that is the real point of Jesus' decision to send them out in pairs. Jesus wanted us all to know that we are not to be Christians in a vacuum, serving alone, praying alone, journeying toward our eternal destiny alone. We need each other, and we were made for a community of faithful, and not as islands in the human condition.

On Friday evening I attended a party and met a lady who, when she learned I was a priest, told me she was Catholic but rarely went to church. She said she was a good person, prayed alone, and tried to do good to others. She then told me a story that she thought was odd. The last time she went to church was to drop off her little niece for a class. She said that they asked her to stay and sit in on a discussion too. She did, and found herself talking quite a bit. To her great surprise, people were impressed and very grateful for what she had to say. She found out that there were people there who needed and wanted her presence.

She thought that praying alone was enough, that she did not need church. But what she learned is this: the question is not if she needs the church; the question is if the church needs her. And the answer to that is a resounding Yes!

We attend church to witness to and support each other in faith. If we think we are so good that we don't need church, then it must certainly be true that others need to see and hear us. Church community is about more than our individual selves - it is about creating an environment of faith where people can experience God's love in and through others. Jesus calls us to be community for each other, not for ourselves. He called us to come together to pray and share. For instance, he said: *For where two or three are gathered together in my name, there am I in the midst of them.* (Matthew 18:20)   Today's gospel further indicated Jesus' desire that we serve together too. We call the reception of Jesus in the Eucharist "communion" for a very good reason - it is the same root word as "community" and indicates our spiritual and real-world unity with the Body of Christ, that is, the people of God.

Our salvation is not about focusing on ourselves, but about focusing on others. We save ourselves by serving and saving others. In bringing Christ to others, we bring Christ to ourselves.

OK, maybe you don't want to pray and serve with others. Maybe you don't want to be in a community of other believers. Look a moment at our first reading today. It is the story of Amos, the early prophet, whom God chose to go and preach to a sinful people. Amos had no interest in serving the Lord, and joining the ranks of the prophets of his day. He did not mince words about it either; here is what he said in our first reading:

"I was no prophet, nor have I belonged to a company of prophets; I was a shepherd and a dresser of sycamores. The LORD took me from following the flock, and said to me, Go, prophesy to my people Israel." (Amos 7:14-15)

Amos did not want to do what the Lord asked him to do. He was content to be a lonely shepherd in the mountains. But he listened to the Lord when asked to get involved. Just like the twelve Apostles did when Jesus summoned them to go out in pairs.

Paul's letter today sums up the reasons why we all need to be like Amos and the apostles, why we can not be solo Catholics or Christians, why we need to work together, serve together, pray together, suffer and die together. Paul reminds us that we have all been blessed with every spiritual gift, chosen by God and destined to know and share in the work of the kingdom. In a nutshell, God has given to each of us a share in the divine life of Christ, what that church document calls "the common priesthood of the faithful." The wonderful gifts we have been given are not for us alone. They are for sharing with others for the sake of the Kingdom. Not to share our faith and Spirit is to waste the gifts of Christ in each of us.

So where does that leave us as a Catholic community in Danville, Virginia? The readings today should strengthen us in our resolve to get involved in the parish life, to recognize our own share in Jesus' priestly mission to the world. May the grace of this sacramental gathering today stimulate each of us to examine our life, our gifts, and to seek actively to share them in the community of the Body of Christ.

A final comment: I hear so often people say how much we need more priests. What they mean is that we need more ordained priests. While this may be true, it can mask the reality that we all can share in the work of Jesus' priesthood, in our own special ways, so that the priesthood of Christ may be more and more available in this and every Catholic parish. It is, from my perspective, time to cease hoping for more priests, and exercise the shared priesthood that we all have been given, in and through Jesus Christ.

Together at Christmas

5th Sunday, B: Mark 1:29-39

When all my daughters and I were together at Christmas of 2001, the last time we all were able to be together, the conversation naturally turned to reminiscing and remembering the past. At one point Elizabeth asked: Dad, we had so many people living with us over the years - strays, foster kids, and others - who was the first person to live with us, and when was that? We all tried to remember who was the first non-related person to come and live with us, but no one could recall. It seemed like there was always someone there in the spare bedroom. But how it all began was a mystery to us all.

It is natural for people to do what my family was doing - to want to know where things came from, or when and how something started. For married couples, questions like that often come from their children and grandchildren: "Mom and Dad, when did you two meet and what was it like?" "Grandma, how did you meet Grandpa?"

Even in church, many ask such questions. I hear them often:

- Where do we get the custom of making the sign of the cross with holy water when we enter church?
- When did the bread we use at Mass look like the pressed white wafers we have today?
- When did the practice of priests not being married begin?

"When did it all begin?" "Where did it all start?" Natural questions, of course. We are naturally curious to know when and how something started. Knowing this type of information helps us to understand things, and to decide how it might affect us in our own behavior.

In today's gospel from Mark, we hear of the end of the first day of Jesus' public ministry. On that first day, Jesus "came to Galilee proclaiming the gospel of God: *This is the time of fulfillment. The kingdom of God is at hand. Repent, and believe in the gospel* (Mark 14b-15). Then Jesus *passed by the Sea of Galilee* and called his first disciples Andrew and his brother Simon Peter, and James and John, the two sons of Zebedee the fisherman (Mark 1: 16-20). Next Jesus took them to Capernaum, and they went into the synagogue where Jesus taught and cured a man possessed by an evil spirit (1:21-28). And that brings us to the late afternoon of Jesus first day of public ministry. We hear in today's gospel what happened next.

Jesus entered the home of Simon Peter and Andrew. It would be a natural thing to do. Simon Peter was from Capernaum. Likely he invited Jesus and his small band of followers to come to his home, get cleaned up and have something to eat. But, upon entering his home, there was a problem. Simon Peter's mother-in-law was quite sick and in bed with a fever. For the Jews, this was fearful. Contagion was expected, and such an illness could be fatal.

Now, these men following Jesus into the house had only just met - and had been impressed with - Jesus. So they must have been watching closely. Jesus, without saying a single word - walked over to the sick woman, *grasped her hand, and helped her up. Then the fever left her and she waited on them* (Mark 1:31).

Finally, after the sun had set, and Jesus was refreshed by food and drink, *they brought to him all who were ill or possessed by demons. The whole town was gathered at the door. He cured many who were sick with various diseases, and he drove out many demons, ...* (Mark 32-34a).

What a busy first day of ministry Jesus had! How very much he accomplished on his initial day of bringing the Kingdom on God to the world!

Well, everything must start somewhere. The glory of Christianity which one day would flower throughout the world through wonderful acts of love and charity began on the very first day of Jesus' public ministry. When did Jesus' actions of love for us begin? When and where was the time when he showed us that we are to take care of our brothers and sisters? Natural questions to ask. Loving others, caring for the sick, helping the less fortunate - it had to begin somewhere. For Christ, it began immediately. From the very beginning, Jesus healed others. From the very first day, Jesus did not wait to be asked to help others. From the start, when Jesus saw someone in need, without a word, he cared for them.

Things always have to start somewhere with someone. How about you? Do you recall the time when, the place where, or the person whom you first reached out to in kindness and charity? Do you remember when your baptismal faith first changed your life from self-centeredness to other-centeredness?

If you don't recall, don't worry. You can do something for others today, and then start counting the memories from this very day. After all, it has to begin somewhere and sometime. Why not now, and why not you?

The Death of Rose

Feast of the Most Sacred Heart of Jesus: 1 John 4:7-16, Matthew 11:25-30

In the last part of the Gospel we are invited to accept the yoke and burden of Christ. He tells us that the yoke is easy and the burden light. I find that hard to accept; and I don't think that many people really believe these words of Jesus either. But that is what Jesus invites us to do: accept the yoke and burden, and then know that they are easy and light.

Perhaps on this wonderful feast of the Sacred Heart of Jesus we can dwell on the meaning of this invitation of Jesus. This easy yoke and light burden is submission to the Father's will. The invitation to submit to the will of the Father stands in contrast to our desire to submit to our own will, needs and desires - that is, to be in control, and to follow our own egos. It is Christ's yoke and burden which is light; it is our own self-imposed burden which is the heavy and difficult yoke.

Even our desires to please God can be a burdensome and weary yoke that far exceeds Christ's burden, a burden that He says is easy and light. Do I find the yoke of Christ easy? The burden of Christ light? Or is it difficult and wearisome? Do I add so much to the yoke and burden of Christ so that it is too hard for me? Is it Christ's burden, or Christ's plus my own self-imposed burden that is heavy and difficult?

The yoke of an animal is something that provides discipline and direction to the animal so yoked. For the Jews in the time of Christ, their yoke was the Law of Moses, given by God to show the people how to conform their lives to the Covenant relationship to God. It was meant to be a joy to be able to know God's will for his people. But the religious sect, the Pharisees, had added more than 200 additional rules to the Law by the time of Jesus, so that this gift of the Law was no longer a joy, but a burden and difficult. And, as we hear so often in the Gospels, Jesus railed against the Pharisees for adding so many extra requirements to the Law. Jesus criticized them for this and accused them for their need to show off their religiousness, with their great pride in the public displays of what they thought were pious rituals. Today, we still have with us the descendants of those Pharisees, but now they are "Christian Pharisees" who make the burden of Christ's yoke wearisome and difficult.

But that is not how Jesus offers us his yoke. The second reading tells us exactly what is the yoke and burden of Jesus - it is Love. Listen again to those words of St. John in the reading: *Beloved, let us love one another, because love is of God; everyone who loves is begotten by God and knows God. Whoever is without love does not know God, for God is love. In this way the love of God was revealed to us: God sent his only Son into the world so that we might have life through him. In this is love: not that we have loved God, but that he loved us and sent his Son as expiation for our sins. Beloved, if God so loved us, we also must love one another.* (1 John 4:7-11)

Two years ago this week, I met a lady who showed me the depth of love for others, a love so sincere, so simple, and so innocent, that she could lift herself right into the most Sacred Heart of Jesus, and find peace, life, and then eternal life. I will call the lady Rose.

It was a Wednesday morning when I was called to the hospital to anoint a lady who was dying, or so I was told. When I got to the hospital I found the lady Rose to be the mother of one of my parishioners. She was from Delaware, but she had gone to Florida for Easter to visit two of her five adult children, and now was stopping off in Virginia to see two more of her children's families. No one told me before I entered her hospital room, but Rose had been in a coma-like state for many days. However, when I entered the room, Rose sat up and greeted me as if she had been dozing a bit. We chatted for a while about her family and her illness. She showed me a book she was reading by an author whom I knew personally; she did not know that the book had been lying there unread for many days, for she did not know of her coma. When I got ready to anoint her and prepare for the Eucharist, I noticed something on the wall at the foot of her bed. There was a very large painting of the Sacred Heart of Jesus. I asked and she told me with eyes gleaming and a bright smile that she was devoted to the Sacred Heart all her life. In his sacred heart, pierced by a sword, she could find comfort; she could give all her own personal burdens into his heart and they did not seem to mean much in comparison. In the Sacred Heart of Jesus, she found rest all through her life.

Rose showed me her Sacred Heart scapular around her neck. Her two sons in the hospital room showed me theirs. The Sacred Heart of Jesus, it seems, was a family affair, in which at least two generations knew and experienced what today's readings are trying to tell us.

But let's get back to Rose. We celebrated the sacraments. I told Rose that the feast of the Sacred Heart of Jesus was in two days, and that I would come back to the hospital and celebrate the feastday Mass in her room, if she were still there. I went out of the room with her son and told him to let me know if she were still alive by then and, if so, I'd be there. He said that all the rest of the children and grandchildren would be here by then, so he hoped she would hang onto life until then.

On Friday morning, no one called. So I took my Mass kit and headed for Rose's room. Sure enough, all the children and grandchildren were there. Rosa was not conscious, however. Still, I set up for Mass on the bedside table, assigned readers and Eucharistic ministers. We celebrated the Mass of the Sacred Heart, the same one we celebrate today. We shared the experience of finding our burdens light, Jesus' yoke easy, when we entered into the Sacred Heart.

As I prayed the Mass, I watched Rose. I did not believe she was unconscious. And, she wasn't! When we joined hands around the bed, hers included, to say the Our Father, her lips moved with ours to the words. I could give her only a few drops of the consecrated wine at Communion. As I ended the mass, saying "Go in the peace of Christ," Rose did just that. She exhaled her spirit and inhaled Christ Jesus eternally.

Rose, you were right. What Jesus said was true, even though it seems hard to believe. When we place our trust in Jesus, when we take his burden on our shoulders, we will find rest. For Rose, it was her faith-filled goal to reach that rest. And she did. Eternal rest in the Sacred Heart of Jesus.

May all who gather here find the same rest by taking on the yoke and burden of the Sacred Heart of Jesus.

Karen's Death

19th Sunday, B: 1 Kings 19, 4-8, John 6, 41-51

It is not about this life. It is about journeying toward God, through this life, into death, and onto eternal life. It is about Jesus' gift of Himself, the Bread of Life that comes down from heaven, as the source of strength and vitality as we move along the journey of life and onto eternal life.

In our first reading, the prophet Elijah figured it out. He was so afraid of being killed by the pagan Queen Jezebel - he wanted to hold onto this life so badly - that he fled the city where the queen was looking for him. He ran into the desert, struggling to save his life. But he could not do it alone. There was no food and no water to be had in the desert. So Elijah lay down to die. He gave up. He despaired of this life. And then it happened.

Once he stopped clinging to this life and to the things of this material existence, he let God into his life. And God came to care for him. Elijah stopped trying to be the one in control; he became utterly dependent on God. The Lord provided for him, and sent an angel to him. Elijah got up and ate once, but was still weak and discouraged. The angel ordered him to eat and drink again. He did so and he was invigorated. Elijah was fed with mysterious bread that restored his strength. With it he could continue his journey to the mountain of God .... *strengthened by that food, he walked fourty days and nights to the mountain of God, Horeb.* (1 Kings 19:8)

Elijah is not so different from the rest of us. We all cling to this life and to the things about us - our family members, our material possessions, our careers, our very selves. There is nothing wrong with caring about the many gifts we have received. But, like Elijah, too strong an attachment to the gifts of creation can cause us to forget the giftedness of the Creator. We can focus so strongly on the things of life that we forget that they are all means to help us journey to eternal life. Moreover, we can come to depend on ourselves, and our own resources so very much that we do not allow for the Lord to be active in our lives.

The life of the Church and of the believers is an exodus, a time of trial, often a crossing of the wilderness. But God remains near those who do not despair of him, even when the burden that crushes them leads them to give up and say, as did Elijah: *It is enough; now, O Lord, take my life,* .... (1 Kings 19:4)

In the gospel, Jesus again offers bread to the hungry, in the form of himself ... *the living bread come down from heaven.* (John 6:51) Jesus is the bread of life, and this bread gives, not human and earthly life, but eternal life. One who eats it will never die.

As a priest, I get to experience many dyings and deaths in my work. It seems that for many people, it is only in the emptiness of dying to this life that they find the fullness and meaning of life. It is in the experience of our mortality that we discover the truth of our immortality. Let me give an example.

When she sent for me, Karen had just been moved into home hospice care. She was given only a few more months to live. Karen had been away from the church for nearly a decade. Like Elijah, she was not ready for death, and she was about to despair; she had been clinging to this life so hard, fighting for a few more days of living so she could to be with her kids. But, like Elijah, she had finally stopped fighting for earthly life. She lay down to die. And she let God come to her to nourish her.

I met her on her back porch. She was using oxygen, a cane, and there were lots of medicines on the table nearby. Although she was weak, she spoke strongly about being tired of living, about wanting to die and get on with it. She had lots of questions about what came after death. After we talked, she was at peace. She invited me to come back soon, and to bring Jesus. I came back the next day. She received the sacrament of reconciliation, and asked for the bread that would give her strength for the journey to the mountain of God. Like Elijah, she needed strength to go on, a strength that could only come from *the living bread that came down from heaven.* It was in the experience of giving up this phase of living that Karen could embrace the next and final phase of eternal living.

I have been bringing Karen the Eucharist now for about three months. This past week I took her that living bread for what I suspect was the last time. How I wish I could share with you the joy she feels in carrying that living bread with her into eternal peace! How I wish I could tell you her words of joy as she prepares to reach the mountain of God! If she could be here, instead of me, she would tell you how the experience of dying and giving up the things of this earthly life has shown her the meaning of life. She would tell you not to miss one opportunity to experience Communion and Christian community.

It is not about this life. It is about dying and rising to eternal life. And the bread that nourishes us on the journey through life, through death, and onto eternal life is here right now. Let us celebrate and go forth to receive that nourishment in this liturgical celebration.

Kenny's Dilemma

21st Sunday, B: Joshua 24:1-2a, 15-17, 18b, Ephesians 5:21-32, John 6:60-69

How often have we been tempted to say, like the followers of Jesus said as they walked away from Jesus: *This sort of talk is hard to endure. How can anyone take it seriously?* (John 6:60) In our faith there are many challenges which arise in Catholic Christianity and Church teachings. Often we don't want to hear them, don't even want to think about why the teachings exist. They aren't what we think, want to believe, or listen too. Consider some of these "hard teachings" of the Church:

- The evils of abortion, euthanasia, and capital punishment;
- The importance of confession of sins;
- Or how about Jesus' teachings?:

> Take up your cross and follow me.
>
> Do to others as you would have them to do you.
>
> Turn the other cheek.
>
> Forgive us our trespasses as we forgive those who trespass against us.

If we are like those who were eagerly following Jesus, we too may be tempted to say: *"This sort of talk is hard to endure! How can anyone take it seriously?"* Those who said that walked away from Jesus, and no longer accompanied him on the journey through Calvary and onto Easter Resurrection.   Maybe there are times when it seems easier to reject what we don't want to hear, in favor of short-term satisfaction. Maybe it's easy to walk away from Jesus and the Church. But, for those who walk away, where is there better to go?

Peter's reply to the Lord makes it clear that there is no other way but the Way of Christ. Even if it is difficult in the short-term, it is the only means of Eternal Life. *"Lord, to whom shall we go? You have the words of eternal life."* (John 6:68)

Which of us doesn't know someone who has left the Church, their religion or religious practices behind? If you consider the number of people you may know who were once active in Church, but now are not, you can probably come up with quite a list. There seem to be so many reasons for walking away from the community of Jesus:

- A priest made me mad by what he said in church;

- The sisters in grade school were mean to me;
- There are hypocrites and sinners in Church, so I do not want to be there;
- I do not agree with something;
- I do not like something - music, times of services, location, decorations, the priest.

Who knows why people walk away from Church? There are so many reasons. It seems to me that people decide, first of all, to leave; then they come up with a reason.

But, OK, even if we can understand why people leave, that does not explain to where they go. It seems that there are many people who walk away from Jesus, and have nowhere else to turn. Is it possible that people walk away from the Church and the community of Jesus, and do not go somewhere else? If not Jesus, then choose someone or somewhere else! In the first reading, Joshua asks the people: *"If it does not please you to serve the Lord, decide today whom you will serve, ... As for me and my household, we will serve the Lord."* (Joshua 24:15) It may have been hard to trust in God when there were enemies waiting to do the people harm, but, as the people responded to Joshua: *... we also will serve the Lord, for he is our God."* (Joshua 24:18)

Let me tell you about Kenny. When he came to see me, he told me he hadn't been in Church in thirty years. He was unhappy; something was missing in his life. While I was helping his sister to die at a very young age, he was struck by her peace and contentment as she faced death. He couldn't understand her peace at first, but then he came to understand it as being related to her faith in the words of Jesus Christ about the surety of resurrection from the dead. That was what he said when he called me; he said he'd do anything for his sister in these, her last days. I suggested that what she would most like is for him to know some of the joy and peace that she already knew; that she would not like him to wait until his imminent death before getting to know the good news of Jesus Christ.

So we talked. Actually, he talked and I listened for nearly four hours. He was angry, sad, hurting. The church had let him down as a youngster. Priests were cruel to him, and he vowed to leave the practice of religion by the time he was 16 years old. That was 30 years ago. And, in those passing years, he did not find anything to replace Christ in his life, and he could not find a way to experience Christ except through a community of faith and, in particular, the community of his youth, the Catholic Church.

So he decided to come home. He was reconciled. He was welcomed home into the loving arms of his Lord. He wept. The Lord wept. I wept. Peter was right. *Lord, to whom shall we go? You have the words of everlasting life.*

As we approach the table of the Lord in this, our parish home, let us all make a promise to go out of here today, and find those who have walked away from Church and invite them to return to a Lord who is waiting to embrace them with loving arms and tears of joy.

Let us share our church community which is so dear to us with all those who have no home in Christ. Let us make all welcome anew in this place.

My First Transfer After Ordination

Pentecost Sunday, C: Mass during the Day: Acts of the Apostles 2:1-11, John 20:19-23

It would be so tempting for me to tell the Bishop that I could not accept his transfer to Newport News and that I simply had to stay here at St. Edwards. I am so happy here, feel a contentment like I have never known before. This is my first home since entering seminary, and it IS home to me. Here is so much love, warmth, acceptance. But I cannot say this to the bishop! I cannot stay here. I have to leave now -- to move onto the next place where the Lord is leading me.

Complacency, that is, spiritual complacency, is a real danger for me, for all of us. Finding a comfortable place is indeed a spiritual goal, and everyone needs to find that comfort. But if the comfort turns into complacency, and a satisfaction with where we are right now, it is a real danger. We stop growing, stop needing God, stop needing to pray and to acknowledge our need for God in our lives.

It is true that not everyone is called to the same things, to the same level of spiritual development. Each of us is different and unique, and can hear and respond to God in our lives differently. What is a complacent position for one may be a real goal for another to achieve. I am not implying that we should not be satisfied or peaceful where we are in our spiritual journey; that would be foolish and would ignore the reality of God's loving grace in our lives. The point is not to be dissatisfied with where we are, but to be peaceful in what we have attained spiritually. But - if we hear God's voice calling us to grow in love, in service, in self -- then to ignore it is to ignore our very selves, and the God which is in us and speaking to us.

Complacency occurs when we reach a level of closeness to God, and want to stop there when we know God wants and needs us to be so much more. That old army recruiting slogan had it right - Be all that you can be!!

In today's readings we hear of the wonderful gift of the Holy Spirit which Jesus sent upon the disciples. There they were, in that small room hiding and afraid. They had watched their leader and Lord leave them. They knew that those who killed him might kill them too. So they stayed in that room, and awaited the promise of the Father - the Spirit.

And then it happened. And they were filled with the Spirit of God and all the many graces and gifts of the Spirit. They were now able to proclaim the good news of Jesus Christ; now they had the ability to go out into the world; now they did not have to fear. BUT, just because they received the Holy Spirit and these wonderful graces, they did not have to do anything about it; they did not have to proclaim the good news. They did not have to leave that secure room.

And we are no different. Just because we received that same Spirit in our baptisms does not mean we have to act on it. We are free to choose to stay in our security or to go out into the world boldly. That's how it is for so many of us. We come regularly to hear Jesus' words; we eat with him weekly; and we feel good about our doing that weekly thing. But -- if it does not impel us to change and to grow in his love, it is not enough to assure us that we shall enter the kingdom of God!

If we have found ourselves becoming very comfortable with where we are as "church," with what we do as Christians, there is danger. Too much comfort, too much security, may imply that we have stopped being challenged to grow in God's love and service.

But, back to me: It is this feeling of security and comfort that I have found here at St. Edward Church. I want to stop, enjoy it, and rest in it. But to do so is to stop following the path of growth in my life -- to become spiritually complacent.

I have a favorite saying from the movies; it was said in "The Sound of Music" by Maria von Trapp as she prepared to leave the security of the Abbey. She is forced to make a decision to stop one part of her life's journey and to begin another, and she is scared. She says: *The Lord never closes a door but that he opens a window.* Well, that is how it is for me now as I prepare to take my leave from St. Edward Church. I must let a door of my journey close, and look out the window. It requires trust in God, and it is a risk. It scares me, but I will do it! To do otherwise would be to resist God's action in my life.

Which of us has not faced the reality that each moment of our life is simultaneously an ending of one journey and the beginning of another? It may be a move from our home, a change of job, a loss of someone to death or transfer, etc. We can look back on the completed part of our journey and be sad, or we can look forward with confident anticipation to the next leg of the journey with gratitude for the past and hope for the future. I choose the latter. I reject spiritual complacency. I want to follow Jesus to Jerusalem, so that I might die and rise with him.

Godspeed to you on your journey beyond Pentecost and into Eternal Life.

I Can't Believe You Are a New Priest!

Nativity of John the Baptist: Mass during the Day: Isaiah 49:1-6, Acts of the Apostles 13:22-26, Luke 1:57-66, 80

Shortly after I arrived here at my new parish, someone who had read that article in the Daily Press about me, came up to me and said: "I can't believe you were only ordained a priest last year. You seem like you were born a priest." My response to him was simply: "I was born a priest. I just did not know it until recently"

And it is true. At least that is how I understand my vocation as a priest. God made me to be a priest. It is what he intended for me. When God was shaping me in my mother's womb, he said: "This one I am making to be a priest." But I had to be born, grow up, gain the right combination of education and life experiences before I could be *the* priest that God needed me to be. God needed a priest of a certain type, and I was formed to be that priest. And, after I had grown and gotten all the experiences of love, and pain, and suffering, and joy, and the education that God needed for this particular priesthood, then God spoke to me and told me to be a priest. But not a second before I had become the person he needed me to be.

When I first became aware of what God wanted for me, I was stunned. I did not want to be a priest. I did not deserve to be a priest; I was not holy, not spiritual, not even a very good person. I had never thought to be a priest. "God," I thought, "You have got the wrong guy!" But God had not made a mistake. So I listened some more. And, after I fully understood what God had intended for my life, I had to make a decision. I was free to say Yes or No. Just like Israel in our first reading, just like John the Baptist in our second reading, just like Jesus' mother Mary, and just like anyone else, I had to make a choice and I was free to say no to God. God loves me so much he gave me freedom to choose.

And I chose to say YES and so you see me here today as a result. It still amazes me to see what and how God wanted me to be. It is so awesome and strange for me. But it fits like a glove; and I am so happy. Now I hope that I can find out why he wanted me to be a priest. Or if not find out, at least be able to be the priest God intended me to be, for whomever God needs to have me serve.

How about you? Would you know it if you were chosen from your birth, and chosen by God to do something in the Lord's plan of salvation?

You are no different from me. So, let me suggest to you that you were. God chose you from your birth to make his Son Jesus Christ more visibly present in the world. Maybe you don't know to whom you were sent; maybe you do not know what message you were asked to bring. Maybe you don't feel worthy to do such a thing. But it is still true. You were chosen by God from your birth, for some role in making God's kingdom come more fully in the world.

Just like we celebrate the birth of John the Baptist today, we should celebrate your birth too. You too are chosen to point to the Lord in our midst. Don't think for a moment that John the Baptist wasn't free to say no to the role that he was given. He didn't have to baptize and preach repentance; he didn't have to point to Jesus as the one whom God had sent. But he did; he freely chose to accept the role for which God had created him, a role not unlike yours, a role to make the reality of Christ more visibly present in our world.

You do not have to accept your role either. You don't have to do a thing that God needs you to do. You don't have to be an instrument of God's love in the world. You are free to choose. BUT, if you haven't already chosen to accept the giftedness of you, the graces God gave you, and the role he needs you to play in the coming of his Kingdom, do it now! Say yes to God; open your heart and let God take over.

I have developed a prayer which I say daily, often many times a day. It goes like this: "Here is my heart, Lord. Here is my mind, my voice and my body. I offer them to you to use for the coming of your kingdom. Please take them and use them as you need. And I will try to stay out of your way as you work." I do not know to whom God wants me to make his love present, but I believe there is someone. If I let God use my hands and heart and voice, God knows to whom He wants to speak, and God knows what to say and how to say it. I do not have to know.

You may think I'm presumptuous but I think I know the meaning of life. When I say "the meaning of life," I mean I know why we exist. I'll tell you why I think we exist.

Consider this. What if the only reason you exist is so that you can make

Christ's love visibly present in the world to one person, for one moment of your life? What if the only reason God made you was so that you could make God visibly present in the world to someone sometime? That would mean you'd spend all your life preparing for that one moment to arrive:
- You'd build up a lifetime of experiences, pain, joy, suffering, and every other thing.
- You'd get an education and a particular understanding of life, and of God, and of your self.

Then, when you'd gotten just the right combination of things that make you the very person God needs to make himself visible, it would happen. There would be one person, someone who'd waited a long time to experience God's love, Christ's presence, in their life, and you'd be just the right combination of things to make Christ visibly present to her or him. You would make God, that is, Love, visibly present in the world to one person.

When that moment passed, you would go through the rest of your life, until the day that God would call you back home with him, having completed the task for which you were made.

If you could really know for certain that you could make Christ, Love, visibly present in the world to one person one time - for sure, for real, for certain - would that not make life worth living? Would that ability to make Christ real for someone not be enough to make all the rest of living worthwhile?

Well, guess what? That is why God made you! You were created to make God's love real in the world for someone sometime.

And in case you do not know it, I am the one person to whom you are making God's love visibly present in the world, right here and right now. I look at you and I see Christ. You were made so that I might experience God's love right now.

But, wait! What if the one person for whom God made you to be the instrument of his love is the person beside you right now? Well, it is. It is.

What if it is the first person you will encounter when you go home today? It is.

What if it is the first person you will meet when you go to work on Monday. It is. It is. It is.

You see, every person and every moment of your life is potentially a moment when you will make Christ's love visibly present in the world to someone. God made you to be just the person you are, gave you the experiences, both difficult and happy, so that you could become you, you who are another John the Baptist, you who have the ability to point to the reality of Christ's love in the world in the here and now.

You may never know just who will be the person whom you may help. You may never know when or how God will use you to show Christ's love. But that is why you were made; that is why you live; and that is the basis upon which you will die and rise with Christ.

Today we celebrate the birth of John the Baptist, called by the Lord from birth, given a name by God in his mother's womb, chosen to proclaim the coming of Christ into the world. Tell me, are you so very different?

Tressa's Letter After 9-11

25th Sunday, C: Amos 8:4-7, 1 Timothy 2:1-8, Luke 16:1-13

I received a letter from my 23-year-old daughter this week. Like most of us, she is thinking about the national crisis and what will occur, and what it will mean. Among those around her are many who are fearful of the loss of their lives and of their possessions, and want retaliation for what they have lost or fear they may lose. While in sympathy with that attitude, she wrote a long reflection on the ramifications of focusing too much on what we have lost. She concluded by writing: "It is not death we should fear, but a life we lead that is less humane."

Our gospel on the unjust steward may shed some light for her, and maybe for all of us as we struggle in our time of national crisis. The gospel parable of the unjust steward is sometimes difficult to read and hear. Jesus actually seems to praise the steward for his dishonesty or "shrewdness." This is especially surprising to find in the gospel of Luke, which preaches the necessity of giving up possessions and even family relationships in order to follow Jesus. But perhaps the message of the story is even more radical than we first expect.

Because he was either incompetent or dishonest with his master's property, the steward was fired. He first responds with panic but then realizes he can turn the situation to his advantage. As the one responsible for holding the receipts indicating the amounts owed by each of his master's debtors, he still wields power. He instructs the debtors, each of whom is no more honorable than he, to rewrite the terms of their agreement with his master. The steward hopes they will be indebted to him when he is unemployed.

This parable of the dishonest steward has to be understood in the light of the Palestinian custom of agents acting on behalf of their masters, collecting fees plus huge interest rates and personal commissions. The dishonest steward who rewrote his master's receipts was writing off his own commission, as well as the interest, it seems. He was foregoing his personal gain, if you will, his commission, for some possible future life. Even the master commends the dishonest steward for thinking about the future, and not being so concerned with today's gains. The parable, then, teaches the prudent use of one's material goods in light of an imminent crisis.

Perhaps the most surprising line in the entire passage is Jesus' recommendation of friendship with such dishonest wealth. Is this the same Jesus who demands that people leave everything behind in order to follow him? Jesus is not commending any dishonesty, but he is reflecting on the proper attitude toward wealth. Whatever the source of wealth, the disciple must be so completely detached from money that its presence or absence is insignificant. What matters is that, what is accomplished - with or without wealth - is of such quality that it will reap an eternal reward. In the end, though, as the final section makes clear, it is important to be detached from the wealth one uses in this world. The purpose of using it is to serve God. Any other goal is idolatrous, placing something material above God.

In light of what Jesus has to say concerning wealth, each of us has to do some hard thinking and sincere praying about our attitude toward material possessions. Money plays such an important role in our daily lives that it influences us deeply, whether we have it or not. In a world where values are out of focus, money talks, opens doors and is a voice that is always heard and listened to. Given the emphasis society places on having lots of riches, it's hard to remain indifferent to its power. Money is something we need, but our need must not turn into a form of worship of money. After all, even our paper bills say "In God we trust," and not "In money we trust." At the end of our life, what will count is the person we are and the good we have done, and not what we have accumulated in material worth.

You already know that, you say. So why do I repeat it here? We are living in a moment in history when the loss of much of our earthly and material goods is a real possibility. As we contemplate our actions and attitudes in the face of such loss, we may look to Jesus' teaching and reflect that all we have, no matter the source, no matter the ownership, is gift of God. And the use of all that we have must be motivated by love of God, and the doing of His will - not by anger or retaliation at material loss, not by hatred. For if we lose our sense of morality and integrity we risk losing much more than our life and our property. We risk losing our humanity.

All over our country in the past days, people are reassessing the meaning of life, of their material goods, and are coming to the Lord. Last weekend churches all across America were packed to capacity and overflowing. In addition, people are sharing themselves with donated time, donated blood, and money and goods, for the sake of people whom they do not know. Out of this time of tragedy, perhaps is coming a renewal of faith and a resurgent respect for others, and an understanding of the proper use of our resources and money. I can only pray that this is not like "January in the gym." Do you know what that means? It refers to the fact that many people crowd into gyms after making New Year's resolutions to get healthy; but it only lasts for the month of January. After that, the gyms have plenty of room.

Perhaps my daughter's concern is ours too - how to do right, without losing our humanity. Let us pray for all who guide us in this time, just as St. Paul tells Timothy, that they may be open to hearing God's will, and courageous in following it, for the good of all and the salvation of the world.

Lord, protect us, protect our families and our country. Let our hearts be open to know and do your will as we struggle in our fears and pain. Give us trust in you, and hope for all peoples.

The Blind Lector

10th Sunday, A: Hosea 6:3-6, Matthew 9:9-13

Sometimes I wish I could be more like Jesus. But then I read gospels like this one, and I wonder if I have the courage to be like Jesus in some ways. This story about Jesus and Matthew, the tax collector who would become an apostle, is incredible.

Of all the apostles, there's none more unlikely to be chosen by Jesus than Matthew. He was a tax collector for the Romans who had conquered the Jewish nation. Himself a Jew, Matthew had gone over to the enemy, to collect their taxes and, in the process, to make himself rich.

It was a challenge for the Romans to develop a way to collect taxes to pay for their conquering army and government in Jerusalem. The method they devised was to auction off the right to collect the taxes in an area. The one who won that right in the auction was responsible to the Roman officials to collect a fixed amount. Anything he could get over that amount was his to keep. You can imagine how much abuse there was in such a system of tax-collecting. With no newspapers or official publications, people did not know how much they ought to pay in taxes. And they had no way to appeal a tax, if they thought it unfair. As a result tax collectors became very wealthy men by extorting, cheating, and dishonest collecting of taxes. The system was so hated and so abusive that, by the time of Jesus, the auctioning off of the right to collect the taxes was ended. However, the hatred of tax collectors still remained strong. And the modified systems for gathering taxes in Jesus' time were not any less corrupt.

When Jesus called Matthew, he was calling a man universally hated. We do not know if Matthew was an honest tax collector; some did exist in theory. But what we see in this story is Jesus' great ability to see into a person's heart, not only what he was, but also what he could become. Unlike the others around him, unlike most of us, Jesus could ignore the outer person and see into the hearts of people. Jesus could ignore a person's reputation or image, and could touch people whom others avoided.

Let's take a look at Matthew and consider what Matthew lost and what Matthew found by responding to Jesus' call: *Follow me.* (Matthew 9:9)

Matthew lost a cushy job, but he found a destiny. He lost a tremendous income, but he found honor. He lost comfort and security, but he found an adventure like nothing he could ever have imagined. Who knows? If we too have the courage to respond to Jesus' invitation to follow him, we'll lose some things too. But there's no telling what bounty and adventures await us if we say "Yes" to Jesus. Not only did Jesus call Matthew, a hated tax collector, Jesus then went and dined with Matthew and his friends. For the Jews of the time, this was a great shock. Jews did not eat food which was not ritually clean; Jews did not associate with sinners, or with those who worked for their Roman oppressors. Jews did not have anything to do with people like Matthew, or his friends. And if Jesus was Matthew's friend, they'd have nothing to do with Jesus either.

Whatever else you may say about Jesus, he was a man of courage. Which of us could reach out to someone in our community whom others avoided, or even scorned? But Jesus had no one whom he avoided or scorned.

I have my own "tax collectors" in my life. We all do. For instance, I used to be uncomfortable around blind people. I felt self-conscious. I didn't know where to look when we were talking. I felt guilty that I had sight and they didn't. It's silly, I know, but it's true, or at least it used to be. Let me tell you about one such person. Leo was a member of my parish. Leo was blind and, in his blindness, he was lonely. So he came to two Masses each Sunday, and he came early and stayed afterward. He would come up to me, to anyone, take hold of an arm, and begin to talk and talk. He was nice too. But I felt uncomfortable and self-conscious with him. So, when he was near me, I would be silent so he would not know I was there. I avoided him.

Then came the third Sunday in Ordinary Time. The first reading was a favorite of mine and I was prepared to preach on it. It was from Isaiah (8:23 - 9:3) and included the wonderful line: *The people who walked in darkness have seen a great light.* To my great surprise when I sat down and waited for the first reader to come forward, who was it but Leo, blind Leo. He was carrying his bible in Braille and he began to read. When he came to that wonderful line, my eyes filled with tears. I think many others did; I don't know because I could not see well through my own teary eyes. Leo was offering himself as a minister in God's service. Leo was putting himself up for possible failure and embarrassment, all for the sake of his love of God.

I could never avoid Leo again. I wanted to touch his arm, to experience Christ as present in him. I wanted to be like Jesus who reached out to Matthew. So I did. As I did so, I wondered how many other people in my life I had avoided, only to miss out on an experience of Christ in the world.

You want to be like Jesus? Then identify the "tax collectors" in your life. All of us have our "tax collectors" whom we avoid. We all know such people; they may be people of different social classes, different nationalities, races or colors. They may be people we took advantage of, gossiped about, cheated, or hurt. Or they may be people who did some bad thing to us. Perhaps today, maybe this week, once you've identified your "tax collectors," let the grace of this liturgy empower you to reach out to one of them. You might be surprised when you do. You might receive an experience of Christ in the world. You may even be a Christ-presence to them. It is so easy to do. Jesus did it. You can too. Be like Jesus. Because Jesus lives in you, and you in Him. Let it be known.

Climbing Mount Snowdon

19th Sunday, A: Matthew 14:22-33

It was the scariest thing I have ever done, maybe the stupidest too. But I did it, and I am here to tell you about it. I climbed Snowdon Mountain in northern Wales while on my vacation last summer. This highest mountain in Wales is one of several which sweep out from the coastal plane into high craggy peaks, with steep slopes and cliffs of 70 to 90 degrees, and drops of more than three thousand feet.

How was I able to do this when I am so afraid of heights, when I had never done such a rigorous hike and climb before? I did it by focusing on the goal, the peak of the mountain, and not focusing on myself, my fears, or the condition of the particular few feet of rock and cliff on which I was presently standing (or more correctly, hanging onto). If I had given in to my fears, if I had let myself concentrate on the absurdly high and steep drops around me, I would have been immobilized. Success involves taking risks - freeing ourselves from the things around us so we can focus on our goal.

For the Christian the goal is Christ. And the only way to make this your goal is to take the risk of faith - the leap of faith in what Jesus Christ taught and did, and promised, and will give. But it is hard to have faith when things are tough. It is much easier to trust in God when there is no need for trust. It is only when great challenges and difficulties come along that our faith is called into question. If you are like most people, it is in such times of challenge that faith is hardest.

In good times we have faith and trust in God. In bad times we assume that we must have faith and trust in our own selves, often wondering why God has abandoned us. Recognizing the presence of God in our lives usually occurs only after the winds die down. In stormy times, our fear and confusion can deafen us to the subtle, quiet ways in which God reveals provident love. Or we can look back at times of turmoil and see that God truly was at work in us even though our distraction kept us from noticing. Maybe that is what happened to Elijah in the first reading. He experienced strong wind, then an earthquake, then fire. Then at last there was a "tiny whispering sound" and it was the presence of God, giving me calm and confidence, after a difficult experience.

In our gospel today, Matthew presents us with Peter in the boat who, once in the water, becomes paralyzed with fear. Notice that Peter was fine as long as he trained his eyes on Jesus and kept moving toward him. But when he looked at the adversity around him instead, he began to sink. But even then, when faith flickers in adverse times, the hand of Christ is there to catch us.

The real miracle in the gospel is the victory over fear and doubt. To be able to trust when it seems impossible, to be able to focus on Christ in difficult times and truly believe that Jesus can and will take care of us. That is the message of the gospel, a message that was hard even for the first disciples to accept.

For the modern Christian, fear can prevent them from truly accepting the message of the kingdom of God and can cause them to keep their hearts tied to what is secure and familiar to them - to be unable to take a leap of faith and jump into the water in order to follow Jesus. For some they prefer their security; it may be wealth, for others, it may be attachments to patterns of life not compatible with being Christian. Rather than generosity and love, small-mindedness or resentments bind their hearts to old hurts. But Jesus challenges those Christians to reflect about their faith and trust only in Jesus and not on material or earthly things.

In contrast, Christian life is characterized by freedom and risk. The Christian is alert and ready to follow the Lord - anywhere, any time, any place. Being a Christian is not about living life half-heartedly but rather living life fully as a gift from God. And that includes taking risks, through a faith which keeps the eyes focused on the source and goal of faith - Jesus Christ.

Today's gospel is about taking the risk of faith; it is about giving up the false security of what we have and are, in order to become what Christ intends us to be and to become. It's like climbing a mountain! Don't worry about where you are and what you have, but concentrate on where you are going, and take the risk to get there.

What are your false securities? Bad habits, prejudices, feelings about self which limit your trying new things. Maybe it is wealth, home, social status, peers, particular automobiles or clothing labels, or a certain life style? A person could find himself or herself in full possession of all their comfortable securities, but no longer be alive, and no longer able to use the many things they have been given as gifts from God, no longer able to become the persons God intended, and no longer able to follow Jesus, even into the waters of life.

If the things you cling to are so wonderful, tell me - which of them can you take with you when you die? How about this? For the ones you can't take with you when you die, why not get rid of them today if they hold you back. If they are gifts, why not use them to help do the Lord's work here and now. I don't mean just money and material things either. You have lots of gifts to share.

Have you ever experienced the loss of a loved one? Why not share this gift with someone else who needs to know how it feels and what faith can mean?

Have you ever experienced a major illness or disease, such as a cancer? Why not share this gift with someone newly diagnosed who is so frightened and alone?

Are you good with kids, or the elderly, or the disenfranchised? Why not share your gifts?

Are you retired, but still full of knowledge and skill? Is there not someone who can benefit from all that God has given you?

Take a risk. Let your faith, not your need for security, guide you today. Trust God, share what you have, with no fear. Remember the goal is Christ. Keep your eyes on the goal, and have no fear. Just like Jesus said in our gospel: *Take courage, it is I; do not be afraid.* (Matthew 14:27)

Tressa's Recurring Illness

All Souls Day, November 2: Daniel 12:1-3, Romans 6:3-9, John 6:37-40

I got a call from my fourth daughter Tressa recently. [Oops! Some of you don't know me and are asking if you are in a Catholic Church - the priest has kids!? For those who don't know me, I was once married, and I have four grown daughters and three foster sons, and I am a Roman Catholic priest.]

I had not spoken with Tressa in a long time, and that itself is a sure indication that there is something going on. But I was surprised when she told me that she was not well - again! She has had Crohn's Disease and ulcerative colitis since she was 13. She has spent a lot of her life in hospitals, on massive doses of prednisone and other medications, until, at the age of 22, she has major surgeries to remove her deteriorated intestines. It was a long process of recuperation and recovery but, after many years of difficulty and pain, the recuperation months seemed like "a piece of cake." And, best of all, at the age of 22, she could finally begin a normal life! The doctors said there was, however, a 5% chance that the disease could recur, though with the removal of all her lower GI tract, they felt confident she would be fine for the rest of her life. Five percent - That means that one in twenty persons with this disease and all this surgery would still be diseased. That could not mean my daughter!

Two years later. It is back. And I have to start again to think about her health, her survival, and her quality of life. I don't like that at all. I have, in the past, considered the possibility of her death. It is not imaginable. Now, if she should have to have more surgery, that possibility of death is, once again, real. I thought we had dismissed that entirely the last time around. I guess I was wrong.

Let me step back a bit, to October 2, 1997. That was the day of my foster son Hieu's funeral. He had been out of the house for over a year, and we had all moved on with our lives. When I got the call two days earlier that he had been killed by a gang, a random act of violence, I was not able to process it. It did not seem real. I went to the funeral, which was preceded by a viewing, as they call it. I could not go up to the open casket. I could not comprehend that it was Heiu in the casket, so there was no need for me to go and look in. Still, when it came time to close the casket for the funeral Mass, I had to go and look. I had to see if it was true. It was true. It was Heiu. He was dead.

Death - It does not seem like a possibility while we are healthy and alive. It does not seem that way with regard to Tressa's disease, any more than it was a possibility for Heiu. Still, it was real for Heiu and it could be real for Tressa. Although I am a strong Catholic Christian, I find that death, as a necessary step to salvation, is very difficult to accept. Life, that is, earthly life, seems to be all there is, although I know better in my heart, giving up this life was not acceptable, not even if the reality of eternal life lay before me and Hieu and Tressa.

When Jesus was a little boy, his mother taught him to say his night prayers, probably not too differently than most of us were taught how to pray by our parents as we knelt beside or sat on the bed. In the time of Jesus, the customary Hebrew night prayer which little children learned was Psalm 31:6. All children learned to say this verse as the last thing before going to sleep. You don't have to go home to look it up; I'll tell you what it is.

As Jesus hung on the cross, his own death imminent, his last words were Psalm 31:6: *Father, into your hands I commit my Spirit.* Jesus said the prayer he learned from his mother, the prayer he always said before going to sleep, just as he prepared to go into the sleep of death. And, just as Jesus awakened each previous day of his life into the community of his family and friends, Jesus knew that on this Good Friday, he would once again awake again into the communion of his family and friends. But this time, his rising would be the glorious Easter Resurrection, by which he overcame death and opened the gates of heaven to all of us.

Just as Jesus died and then arose again to new life, so too do we understand that all who share in the life of Christ through Baptism, will also share in the sleep of death, and then rise anew to new life in Christ. We too will awaken to the communion of saints.

Life is a journey toward death. Our lives which begin with our conception start a journey of return to God. We understand our growth in the life of Christ to begin with our baptism, when we die to sin, and are born to a life of faith in Jesus Christ. From the very moment of our baptisms, it is our hope and our goal to return to be with Christ. From that perspective, death is a goal of life, a death which begins an eternal life with the Lord.

Still, we know that death is real, but that it is, for the one who lives with faith in Jesus, merely a dying to this life in order to rise to new and eternal life, where there is no dying, no suffering, only goodness. And I know that this is just what Jesus wants for all of us, for family and friends, for me and for you. And I know too that Jesus showed us the way to this goodness. For he too suffered and died and rose to eternal life. And that makes it my eternal life too. And yours.

That is why it is good on this feast of All Souls to reflect on the reality of dying to this life. That is why we pray for all the souls who have died today. Jesus said it best in today's gospel from John: *For this is the will of my Father, that everyone who sees the Son and believes in him may have eternal life, and I shall raise him up on the last day."* (John 6:40)

So, despite the fear of death, our consolation is the knowledge that we can share in Jesus' rising to eternal life.

Bread Offering in Romania

The Dedication of the Lateran Basilica: John 2:13-22

I wonder how Jesus would have felt if those sellers of animals and food were not accepting any money for their things. I mean, what if those guys with the money, the animals, and other things had brought them to the temple to give away, instead of to sell them? Just like some people bring food to church so that it can be given to God's Storehouse, to distribute to the poor. What if these people in the gospel had brought their things to the Temple to offer to any who would be in need, or hungry, or poor? I think Jesus would have felt differently then, and our gospel would not be about Jesus driving them out, but about Jesus inviting them in. Something like that occurred in a church I visited this summer on vacation.

While I was on vacation visiting a priest friend in Romania, I had the opportunity to celebrate Mass with my friends there. On a Tuesday morning in Bucharest, the capital city, I joined two other priests in celebrating morning Mass (for a packed church, by the way!). After the Communion Prayer, my colleague Father Lucian motioned for me to move from behind the altar down to a corner of the church, to an area where there was a statue of St. Anthony of Padua. He said that I should just be quiet and listen to the prayers (which, of course, I would not understand at all, since they were in Romanian!).

When we walked to the area, I was surprised to find baskets and bags containing loaves of freshly baked bread there. There were so many; I was amazed that I did not notice them before, if not by sight, then certainly by the wonderful aroma. While I stood there in front of this mountain of bread, one of my priest colleagues prayed, sprinkled holy water, and recited what appeared to be a litany. Then, just as unexpectedly as we went there, we returned to the altar for the final blessing.

After Mass, when I got back into the sacristy, I could hardly wait to ask what that was all about. Father Robert told me that it was a local custom that, on each Tuesday morning, people who could afford it stopped on the way to Mass and bought fresh bread - as much as they could buy and carry. They brought it to church and placed it there in front of the statue of St.

Anthony. The bread was blessed and left there for the rest of the day. Anyone who was hungry, or who could not afford to buy bread, was free to come and take it. And there were many poor there.

I went back out on the altar in time to watch one woman. She took back the bag of bread she had brought, and distributed it in the back of the church to some very needy old men, who seemed too feeble and too embarrassed to come forward.

Later in that day, we were visiting the cathedral of the diocese of Bucharest. There too, in front of a statue of St. Anthony, was bread, one loaf of bread still not taken.

My American colleagues who were traveling with me were as impressed as I was with the bread blessing and distribution. They asked me if I would consider doing something like that back in my home parish, not bread but perhaps food and other things. My first reaction was a resounding "yes." But, after a short reflection, I thought otherwise. If people brought food and left it for blessing and then free distribution, someone would come and take it all, or others not in need might steal it. Further, I suspected some others would complain about the clutter, the unwelcome traffic in the church, and the security risks involved. And they would be quite justified in their concerns. Finally, I wondered if really needy people would come to the church for their need. In the end, I thought it a beautiful custom, but one that is appropriate only for Romania.

But, I do wonder .... Wouldn't it be nice to live in a society where such a custom could be done? Not that I would wish that there were hungry people. But that people came to church to offer things from their bounty? Like time, talent, or treasure?

This weekend we celebrate Stewardship Sunday, a time to reflect on the many gifts we have - our talents, our time, and our treasure. It is time to bring our gifts to the parish community and to give them away. We are not to sell them; that is not what Jesus wants, as our gospel indicates. But we sell our gifts when we ask for something in return - for admiration; accolades or honor; recognition or respect. We sell our gifts when we give them out of a sense of forced duty or obligation, that is, in order to avoid feelings of guilt or shame. That is not what Jesus wants. To sell our gifts in that manner is to invite Jesus to drive us out too. Instead, we give our gifts of

time and talent and treasure freely:
- because it helps the work of Jesus;
- because we have much to give;
- because all we have has been given to us freely from God.

We give of ourselves because Jesus gave of himself, and then invited us to do the same.

As you leave today, please stop at the tables in the Commons, and consider all the many ways you can offer some of yourself for building up the Kingdom of God here. If you cannot offer your time or talent, consider offering more of your treasure. If you cannot offer anything at this time, then pray for our parish community. Pray that others who are more fortunate in what they have been given by God will be generous in their giving.

Often in the gospels, we hear Jesus call forth children and the young to show us how we are to live as followers of Jesus. At this time, I would like you to hear about our school children and their wonderful example of sharing of their time and talents with others. [Introduce the school principal who will introduce the student government officers who will tell of the Mustard Seed project in which each class has adopted a community organization for the past year, and donated their time, talents, and money to help. The school received the diocesan award for outstanding service program.]

Death of an Eight-Week-Old

The Solemnity of Christ the King, B: Revelation 1:5-8, John 18:33b-37

Jesus answered, My kingdom does not belong to this world .... (John 18:36a).

Nine days ago I did a funeral service for an eight-week-old baby. It was a sad experience for me. All I could do was say the words, and move on. There was nothing that could console the parents, especially the father who was responsible for the freak accident that resulted in the untimely death. My only hope was that the words I said brought an experience of Christ, if not then, perhaps later. But not too much later, I hoped.

I am sure that the death certificate listed the cause of the infant's death as a "brain hemorrhage" or a "traumatic concussion" or some other fancy way of saying that the baby had an internal head injury and bled to death. But, no matter what was listed as the cause of death, I can tell you what was the real cause of the baby's death. And it was not something that a doctor would put on a death certificate. The cause of death was poverty. Just like the two other babies I have buried since coming to this city, the baby died due to the poverty of the family and situation into which he was born - a condition of deprivation that makes living an impossibility for some babies. For me that realization only made the experience of the funeral more pathetic.

But, let us not get off track and forget that today is the feast of Christ the King. Christ reigns over all, yesterday, today and forever. As we heard in the second reading from Revelation: "I am the Alpha and the Omega," says the Lord God, "the one who is and who was and who is to come, the almighty." (Revelation 1:8) Yes, on this last Sunday of the church year, we pause and contemplate the reality of Christ as King over all that is, was, and will be, as the One who will come and rule eternally. The first reading from Daniel portrays God as king of all kings, ruler of all rulers, and power of all powers. We give thanks to God for the gift of his Love, in the knowledge and experience of His Son, as we celebrate Christ as our King and Ruler.

But, at the same time, I am wondering about that family whose child I buried nine days ago. I wonder if they know that Christ is King of kings and Power of all powers. I wonder if they experience Christ's power in their lives. It does cause one to wonder where is Christ in such a tragedy. And, as in so many difficult situations, I hear others wonder where is Christ, the all-powerful one, in their own tragedies.

On this feast of Christ the King, we are given an answer to that question about the presence of the all-powerful Christ in the world, and in our lives, no matter the conditions of that life.

When Pilate questioned Jesus about being the King of the Jews, Jesus told him (and us too): "My kingdom does not belong to this world ...." (John 18:36) That is the crucial point: Jesus is not an earthly king, whose power is limited to earthly matters, or whose followers are limited by earthly matters either. Jesus is not an earthly ruler whose energies are directed toward the finite and temporary. His followers do not expect to find Christ's perfected Kingdom in the material and mundane of earthly living, but in the building up of the Body of Christ into the Kingdom of God, by imitation of Christ - through living, suffering and dying, and then rising to new and eternal life with the eternal King.

I don't believe that Christ intended that we be free of suffering. Jesus suffered, and I believe he suffered, not to save us from suffering, but to show us how to endure suffering. For he knew there was no life without suffering.

So, where was Christ on that day of an infant burial, nine days ago?
- He was there in the suffering of the parents, uniting them to his own suffering, and thereby giving them assurance that suffering will eventually lead to new life.
- He was there in the dead body of the baby, shining out of the beauty and innocence of one so young, one who attained eternity with only a short pause on earth.
- He was there in the words, the hugs and kisses, and the tears of the friends and family, whose very love made the Love which is God ever real for the family.
- He was there in the prayers which I said and which were repeated, as we acknowledged the greatness of Christ our King whose Kingdom is not of this world but whose Kingdom is meant for all of us, even that infant.

So where is Christ in the fullness of his kingdom? He is where that little baby is; he is where so many of our friends and family have gone. He is reigning in the Communion of Saints. Christ is the King of Kings. But his kingdom is not of this world. His invitation to his kingdom is made to all. Christ has expended much love and effort to help us all achieve that Kingdom. He showed us by his own death that we are not bound to the things of this world. The accidents of this earth have little to do with our getting home to share in the Kingdom.

There are some who would have Christ make this earthly place more perfect, more wonderful, so that they might not desire to move onward to the eternal kingdom. But should Christ limit his kingdom and power to this earth, in the here and now? No, his reign must be everlasting and all in all. He will make all this into his heavenly kingdom when he returns in glory. But until then, he prepares his perfect kingdom, not of this world, for all of us.

Let us rejoice in Christ our King, our Savior who came to give us life, and will come again to give us eternal life. Let us keep our focus on his Kingdom as our lighthouse and beacon unto eternity.

Dad's Cancer Diagnosis

Christmas Mass at Midnight: Isaiah 9:1-6, Titus 2:11-14

Life is too short.

Last week my father was diagnosed with cancer. It was a very scary moment when Mom told me. And I could tell she was scared too. My Dad's brother died in 2001 with this same kind of cancer and, many years ago, his father died of it too. So there has always been a fear and anticipation that Dad might get it some day too. And now it has happened and he has the cancer.

Dad's diagnosis resulted in many phone calls and e-mails among the members of my family, as we discussed the meaning of this event, and how we might respond with love and support and caring. We talked through the various scenarios and began to make tentative plans in the back of our minds for things that we were not quite willing to say out loud.

For all of us, this knowledge brought to mind many memories of Dad, of how hard he has worked to care for our family, and how good he has been to Mom in supporting us. It was Dad who brought to our family the gift of the Catholic faith. It was Dad who instilled in us a deep knowledge and respect for our Bavarian heritage. And it was Dad who, by his diligence and hard work, showed his children how to be strong and persevere in accomplishing many things in life. We owe a lot to Dad, and this difficult diagnosis has helped us to remember and reflect with love and gratitude.

For me personally, I am more like my father in intellect, appearance and disposition than I am like my mother. I owe Dad a great deal in terms of the size of his contribution to my genetic pool. I am also indebted to Dad for the roots of my priesthood in the Catholic faith. During this past week, many thoughts like this have gone through my head. It is for me, like so many people, that we become more appreciative of someone or something when we realize that we will not have that person or thing forever, that the time of their being with us is limited. The gift of a father's love in our lives becomes more apparent when we take the time to reflect and ponder that person.

So too with Jesus. Today we celebrate again the birth of Christ, that moment when God the Father sent his Son to live with us, to teach us how to live and love, to invite us to be with him eternally, and to grow to fullness of Spirit on the way to that eternal reunion. It is a time of year when we focus on the Father and the wonderful gift of his Son Jesus - At least that is what we hope most people will do: remember the wonderful gift that Our Father gave us 2000 years ago, and then celebrate the fact that the Gift is still with us, and will always be if we choose to follow Him.

Why do I tell you all this? Because, for too many, once Christmas is over (and, for some, that will be in about 24 hours), they forget about the amazing and most wonderful gift of Christmas, the gift of Jesus. Until another year rolls around, they "Put Christ in Christmas," and nowhere else. Except, of course, if they should be facing the possibility of death during the year. Then too they remember Christ, and the wonderful things He brought us and made possible.

It seems a shame that it takes an annual event like Christmas or the possibility of death for us to take the time to appreciate our gifts.

Christmas is about a Father's love for his children. It is about a Father who loves his family so deeply that He would give himself to them, that He would come and be born in a muddy and dark barn, assume a most humble existence, and then give His very life for those he loves. Christmas reminds us too of the love our own fathers and mothers, and all who help us to know and have life. It seems a shame that we express our love and gratitude in return for this wonderful gift of a Father's love annually, instead of daily, or better.

Don't wait until Christmas to tell Our Father of your gratitude for his wonderful gift of love. Make your gratitude for the One who is the true Christmas Gift a daily expression. After all, does Jesus come to you annually, or daily?

It is not just Jesus who deserves our constant love and appreciation. Did not Our Father give us many people in our lives whose love shows us a bit of God's own love? Don't wait until Christmas to say "thank you" to them either. Sure, an annual card or gift is fine. But is not a frequent call, visit, or note an even better way to express gratitude?

Don't wait until another year goes by before you give thanks for the many gifts of a Father's Love. Life is too short. I know. Dad knows. And now you know too.

Jesus Is Abandoned

Passion (Palm) Sunday, A: Isaiah 50:4-7, Philippians 2:6-11, Matthew 26-27 The Passion of our Lord, Jesus Christ

If you had been there on that terrible and frightening evening in the garden, or in the courtyard of Pilate, or standing along the way to the hill of crucifixion, or even looking on at Jesus, tortured, crowned, and pierced with nails as he strangled on the cross, ...

If you had been there, what would you have done?

Would you have fallen asleep in the garden of Gethsemane?

Would you have stood still while Judas kissed him?

Would you have followed the mob who took Jesus into the courtyard?

Would you have denied knowing him?

What would you have yelled out? "Crucify him!" Or "We want Barabbas"?

If you saw Jesus fall three times, would you have come forward to carry his cross?

Would you have looked down or turned away, lest you be dragged into helping this Jesus?

Would you have had a turn as casting the lots for his clothing?

Honestly, what would you have done for Jesus that day?

If you cannot think of anything, then maybe that explains why it is still so easy to do nothing.

But it is not too late.

Come and walk with Jesus this week. Be there for him, for yourself, on Holy Thursday, on Good Friday, and the Easter Vigil. Pray and stay close to him. This week you have another chance. Do not let him be abandoned again.

I Love My Priesthood!

Easter, Mass of the Day: Luke 24:1-12

If you are under the age of about ten, Easter joy means candy. Lots and lots of candy. So let's talk briefly about candy and what it means to a child.

If you lock a child in a candy store for a weekend, you have no right to complain that he or she eats too much candy.

If you give a person a job to do which he loves to do and is incredibly devoted to, you can't complain that he or she is a workaholic.

If God calls a man to priesthood when he is nearly fifty, you can't complain that he works too much in his parish.

It just isn't fair. Kids love candy, many people love their work, and this man loves his priesthood.

I am here today to say that I love my work, that I am honored to be called to serve my God, by serving his dear children, and that I don't apologize for my gusto or my energy in doing so. I came to the job late in life, as was God's plan for me. And I have lot of catching up to do; there is much time to make up. So don't criticize me for working too much. I am like the kid in the candy store, like the child with the newly found Easter basket. Except that, unlike the child, you can not take me away from the candy. Even if I wanted you to. Which I don't.

In telling you this, my only hope is that you are envious of me, having something to do which I love doing. Working with the gifts God has given me, and nothing else. Doing what I can for the good of God's kingdom.

But such a position as I am in has its risks too. Committing to follow Christ, loving the opportunity to do so, means following Christ in all things. It means: Knowing that I will be able to follow Christ into suffering. Knowing that I may have to die in what I am doing. ["Father Charles," Mike said to me. "If you don't slow down, you could die." And I replied: "What a way to go!"] Following Christ means feeling good about giving my all in order to have the opportunity to share in his Passion and death. But it is all worth while. For it means also sharing in his resurrection. That is exactly why we are here this evening/morning.

I am a lucky guy. I have found my calling, and I love it so much I can die doing it, with confidence in the meaning of dying to self and dying for Christ. People shouldn't criticize me or anyone else who has found God's plan for their lives. They should, instead, rejoice for us, and with us. We have found our niche, and we are so happy.

Is your lack of enthusiasm for me an indication that you are a bit jealous? Because you don't love what God has given you to do? Or because you are not working for God's kingdom? Because you are working for yourself and your needs?

Easter is a reminder to us each year of the meaning and goal of our living. It is to imitate Jesus in his suffering for others, his dying for love of others, so as to rise eternally with God. Life is about God, and God's plan for each of us. Easter makes a bold statement in contradistinction to the day-to-day false images we receive that we are to live for today, for ourselves, for what we can accumulate in the here and now.

It is not too late to join me in my joy. It is not too late to enter your own personal candy store and relish all that is there. Tell the Lord what you need. Ask the Lord what he needs. Then go do it. Get into the candy store and eat your heart out. Maybe then you will have made room in that heart of yours for Christ.

Would you not like people to come to your grave, after your death, only to discover that you are not there, but that you have risen with Christ. Would not you love to have those words of the gospel said of you: *"Why do you seek the living one among the dead? He is not here, but he has been raised.*

It is not too late to change. Your time of resurrection is not here yet. Or is it?

She Stays Away from the Eucharist.

5th Sunday of Easter, C: Acts of the Apostles 14:21-27, John 13:31-33a, 34-35

By the time the early Christian church reached the point that is described in our first reading today, some of the original zeal of the apostles had probably begun to fade a bit. In many of the new churches which were developing, already there was arguing and bickering about whether the new Christians had to obey the Mosaic Laws of the Jews too, or if they could be discarded. They argued over whether Christianity was a new branch of Judaism or a completely new religion. There was arguing over which of the Apostles was really the leader of the fledgling church. There was arguing too among the communities about whether each one was getting a fair share of the collections.

As if that were not enough, the Romans were still around, and growing increasingly hostile toward this new religious sect of followers of the Christ. And soon there would be persecutions of Christians.

So, in the first reading we see that Paul is now beginning to cajole the Christian communities, to urge them to practice another virtue, the virtue of perseverance. We read: *They strengthened the spirits of the disciples and exhorted them to persevere in the faith,* .... Perhaps that is the very best that can be said about any of us.

Christ tells us in the gospel that we are to love one another as He loved us. But, for most of us, loving others is not easy and, at times, it is impossible. When we find that we cannot feel love toward another, when we feel that we cannot even tolerate someone, we may be drawn to despair. To give up. To walk away from Christ. It is indeed hard to persevere.

I have a friend Catherine who has not gone to Communion for years because she is angry with a family member. She can not get over this anger, this hurt, and so she will not experience Christ in the Eucharist. I cannot convince her otherwise either. But I am praying that Catherine goes to church this weekend, wherever she is, and that she hears Paul's exhortation to the early Christians. It was not easy for them to persevere in faith, and it is not easy for any of us at times. What is important is that we recognize that Jesus is patient in his persevering love for us. For certainly, Christ loves us with great persistence. He was, after all, a human being like all of us, with every human feeling and emotion, and he was surrounded by people who showed him misunderstanding, hostility, ingratitude, and plain ordinary stupidity. There must have been the temptation to give up too. But he did not. He persevered in his love, even when most difficult.

His lesson gave the early Christian church its model. As we heard Paul say to the struggling early church in the first reading: *"It is necessary for us to undergo many hardships to enter the kingdom of God."*

Long ago my friend Catherine was a little girl, dressed in a white dress and maybe a veil. She prepared and studied, and waited with great anticipation for the day of her first communion. What wonder must have been in her heart that day! Maybe you can recall your own first communion day and how you felt. Consider how far astray Catherine has gone, to allow her bad feelings to become greater and more important than that wonderful feeling of Jesus' coming into her heart. Whatever went wrong that Catherine chooses (yes, chooses) to hold anger in her heart so strongly that she can not make room for Jesus anymore?

It was the night before his death. Jesus was sitting with the disciples at dinner. Judas got up and left. Jesus knew that the goal of his real mission to the world had come. What were his first words: *My children, I will be with you only a little while longer. I give you a new commandment: love one another. As I have loved you, so you also should love one another.* He called them "my children," with deep love, and told them that he would not be with them much longer. So he told them his most important message - *Love one another. As I have loved you, so you also should love one another.*

Are we so different? We too will not be around much longer - for some, a few decades; for others, a few years, for some, less than that. Life is too short to fill it with anger, with hatred, with unforgiveness. Life is too short to waste it on the petty of earthly life. Life is a short preparation, indeed, for some, a trial. But it is about preparing to share in the Eternal Gift of God, Perfect Love. So it is only natural and reasonable that we who want to share Eternal Perfect Love should practice love and the one best way to spend our lives on earth.

If you are like my friend Catherine, pause and listen to Paul's words about perseverance in times of difficulty. Hear Jesus call you "my child" as he was dying to show you his love. Then go out and love one another.

I Did Not Speak Spanish When I Came Here.

Pentecost Sunday, C: Mass During the Day: Acts of the Apostles 2:1-11, John 20:19-23

When I came to Sacred Heart parish two years ago this week, I did not know how to speak Spanish. But I was about to get on a fast-track to learn. Immediately I had to celebrate the sacrament of Reconciliation in Spanish, Mass in Spanish, and, much to my surprise, I had a difficult funeral Mass to do for a two-year-old boy, with all the pastoral care that goes with it, and all in Spanish.

From the very first day I got here, I have been trying to learn Spanish. To make myself grow, I decided to do everything that a pastor should do in Spanish. I had to try to read everything - prayers, songs, the Mass, even the homily - and the strangest thing was that I had no idea if anyone could understand me when I tried to speak Spanish. Much of what I read I did not understand. I am sure that it was as difficult for the people to understand me as it was for me to pronounce some of the words! I felt a lot like those people in our first reading at the Tower of Babel, babbling away with strange and useless sounds. I still celebrate all the sacraments in Spanish regularly. But to this day, I still don't know if they can understand me. Still, each week, I celebrate Mass and read my homily in Spanish, without knowing if I am understandable at all.

On that first Pentecost, when the Apostles were filled with the Holy Spirit, they began to speak in many different languages. I don't suppose it was much different for them as it is for me. Did the Apostles know if the people could understand them when they were speaking words that they themselves did not understand? Did the Apostles even know what they were saying as they spoke, through the power of the Holy Spirit, in so many different languages? But, not being able to know if they were making sense, they still continued to proclaim as the Spirit moved them. That is quite amazing, you must admit!

Without knowing what they were saying, without knowing if they could be understood, they continued to speak. They are my inspiration each weekend when I get up to celebrate Mass in Spanish for our hundreds of

Hispanic Mass attendees. Perhaps they should be an inspiration to all of us who believe we have received the same Holy Spirit in our baptisms and confirmations. I don't mean an inspiration about our being able to speak in foreign languages. I mean that they are an inspiration and role model for all of us who find it hard to let the Spirit of God that is in us be in control of our words and actions.

Do you ever find yourself worrying about what other people think of you, of how you dress, where you live, who you are, or what you do? Are you a person who is strongly influenced by others' opinions about you? Maybe you work hard to try to please others, by conforming to their expectations for you, that is, by doing what they want you to do, rather than what your good judgment or conscience might tell you. If so, you may find strength in the ability of those first Apostles at Pentecost. They did not worry about what others were thinking, hearing or expecting. They were aware that the Spirit of God had come into them. So they were bold in what they did. They were true to the Spirit in them. Knowing that they were doing God's will, even if they did not understand how or why, they did it. They opened their mouths and gave witness to Jesus Christ.

And don't forget that Jesus told them that they would be persecuted for preaching his name and good news!

So too can it be for all of us. If we are true to the Spirit of God in us, we do not need to be bothered about pleasing others, or letting others' expectations for us, affect what we do and say. If we know that we are living as God intends us, we can be bold in how we live, in how we speak, and what we do.

The ultimate test of how we live our lives is that we live every moment with the sure knowledge that our God is there with us, hearing, watching, seeing, guiding and loving us. If we can feel good knowing that God is standing with us in all we do - watching us, hearing us, touching us - then we know that what we are doing is God's will. So we can do it with the same boldness of the Apostles that Pentecost day.

Sometimes doing the will of God means simply letting the Spirit take control of us. Relying instead on our own will or, worse still, on the will of those around us for our guidance can lead us, and others, away from God.

If the Apostles had the courage to let the Holy Spirit take control of them that first Pentecost, even though they did not know what they were saying or how, then how much easier it ought to be for each of us to let the Holy Spirit take over in us who know and understand what God intends for us to be and do.

When they don't know what to do, some people ask the question: "What would Jesus do?" The answer to that question for those who ask, and even for those who do not ask, is simple. Jesus is living in us and will guide our actions and words if we let his Spirit work in us. What would Jesus do? Open your heart, forget yourself, and find out!

I Will Speak Anywhere, To Anyone.

14th Sunday, C: Luke 10:1-12, 17-20

A couple of months ago, I was invited to give a talk to the Rotary Club about some of my life experiences. I was hesitant to accept because I could not tell them about myself, who I was, and what the life experience meant, unless I told them about Jesus Christ and the gospel. Since the Rotary is a non-sectarian group, I wasn't sure how to give the talk. But, I wanted to do it, and so I prayed about it. Then I went to the lunch meeting and waited to be called to the speaker's podium.

I told them my stories, and I did not shy away from how my life has been a journey of discovery of what God was preparing me to do for Him. While trying to respond to the Rotary request to speak of my foreign travels, I told them instead of my spiritual travels. To my great surprise, they loved it, and they thanked me.

Then I was asked to be the speaker at the Annual Foster Parents Meeting in this area. I was to speak of my life as a foster parent. But I was once again hesitant because I could not say who I was as a foster parent, what being a foster parent did to me, and how it was part of who I am today unless I was prepared to tell them about the meaning of love, of investment of self in others, and how doing those things was following the gospel of Jesus Christ. But I prayed again, and I went and gave my talk about being a foster parent. That is, about being a foster parent because Jesus commands us to love the children, invest in them, and teach them of His love for them. I wore my clerical clothes, just as I did at the Rotary, and I was a bit afraid. But I did it, and I got a standing ovation - twice.

Now, I am not telling you these things so you know I get around town, or so that you think I am a good or popular, speaker. No, you can judge that for yourself if you come here regularly and hear me. I am telling you about these events because they demonstrate how hungry people are for the Word of God in their lives. I am telling you this because my role in speaking to these people was not because I was a priest, not because I was a Catholic or a Christian, but because I was a guy who had lived life and, in the process, had found and experienced some interesting things. That is, I was invited to be myself, not my profession, not my career, not my education, but simply myself. And in being myself, I have found in living the joyous experience of the reality of Christ among us, journeying with us always, even in the strangest of circumstances. In that sense, I am not any different from you or anyone else.

People are hungry for the gospel. People want and need to hear that Christ can be found in the ordinary, and the extraordinary, events of life. My fear in speaking to the Rotary, the Foster Parents group, or anyone else is a reflection of my lack of courage in being who and what God made me. Like most people, I find it hard to preach Christ to strangers. It is not easy to let our Christian spirit show through us. For many, or maybe for most, we try to hide our faith, and put it on like a suit of good clothes, only on Saturday night or Sunday morning. And when we leave the church, we remove external trappings of our faith.

But Jesus calls for boldness in proclaiming him to the world. And he calls on everyone to do it, anywhere, any time, even to the Rotary Club in Danville, Virginia.

Today's gospel describes how Jesus sent his disciples out to prepare for his coming by giving them "travel tips" for their missionary journey. A careful look at it is revealing. For instance, Jesus sends out seventy-two disciples. The people of the time of Jesus believed there were seventy-two nations in the world. So, sending out seventy-two meant that all the nations of the world should receive Jesus' teaching.

Next, we note that he sent them out in pairs. We are not meant to build the body of Christ on earth alone. We are meant to work with others; we are meant to be in communion with others. That is part of the reason why it is not sufficient for a person who calls himself a Catholic to stay home on Sundays, and to pray alone. We are to build a community, a communion of common faith, through praying together, working together, serving together, and growing together. A disciple of Jesus is a brother and sister to others, in a very real sense. Who are you walking with on this faith journey? Are you a help or a hindrance in their progress in faith?

Next, in his travel tips to the disciples he sent out, Jesus advised against any extra baggage, any extra clothing. You can't get very far when you travel if you take along a lot of baggage. That is as true today for the vacationer, as it is for the missionary follower of Jesus. Besides, taking a lot of things on our life's journey only focuses us on those things, and causes us to spend our energy on amassing material things, and then on protecting them so they grow. Jesus told them to carry no money bag, no sack, no sandals, lest they get in the way. What are you carrying that is slowing you down from making progress in your faith journey?

Finally, he gives them a very ominous warning that they are sent as lambs among wolves. Not exactly reassuring words for timid fishermen and shepherds. Their guidelines were simple: go where they were received (verses 5-6); remain in one place (verse 7) and eat what was set before them (verse 8). This would help them avoid the appearance of being mercenary. The basic idea behind Jesus' instruction is that his disciples were not to depend on anything or anybody except on the Holy Spirit of God. Jesus told his disciples to avoid the appearance of being mercenary. What would he tell you? How dependent are you on material things or on making money?

But there is reason for much comfort in all this sending out of the first seventy two of Jesus' disciples. The mission of the seventy-two disciples was not a human project. They could rely on God to take care of them, IF they had the courage to take the risk of trusting Jesus. Jesus knew they would need strength. That is why he gave them his Body and Blood, his written word, and his Spirit. In proclaiming the good news of the kingdom, they were not alone, or even in pairs. They were partnering with God himself in God's work. It is the Lord who is working in and through us. Therefore, constant contact with the Lord of the harvest is necessary. We must, then, be men and women of prayer - not only an hour a week at Mass but on a daily basis. How do you keep in touch with the Spirit of God in you? If you are not in close touch, how can you let the Spirit shine out from you?

Most of those first disciples who went out and obeyed Jesus boldly in proclaiming his message were eventually killed as martyrs to the faith. I guess that is the real message of this gospel. The world needs martyrs for the faith still. And the world loves a martyr. I don't mean a martyr who has to be killed by a sword, a hungry lion, or any other physical death. The world needs martyrs who are willing and able to sacrifice themselves and their material and emotional needs for the sake of Christ.

A modern martyr has the courage to stand in front of strangers and tell of his faith in Jesus Christ.

A modern martyr has the humility to let others see in her simple life the active presence of the Holy Spirit.

A modern martyr looks just like me, or you, or the person beside you.

Why not take the risk of dying to self so as to rise to Christ?

Which of the Men Are You?

15th Sunday, C: Luke 10:25-37

Four men in our gospel.

The first man: He was just going down the road of life when he was suddenly beat up and left for dead. It could happen to anyone.

You might criticize him for traveling that winding, hilly and difficult road. It was known to be a dangerous place to travel, even in modern times. And you could even criticize him for traveling alone. He should have known better, you could argue. And you may be right too. But being right about him or, knowing he did something foolish, doesn't change the situation. He's near to death, beat up, and hasn't a penny to his name. So whether he was foolish or not doesn't change things. Even if he did a stupid thing by traveling the road alone, he still deserves to be helped, don't you think?

The second man: He was just going down the road when he saw a man on the side of the road and left for dead. It could happen to anyone.

He was on his way to Jerusalem. He was a priest and was probably heading for an important gathering in the temple. He couldn't be late. He had put on his good clothing too, and he couldn't let them get dirty by stopping to help the man lying along the road. Besides, maybe the man lying there was ritually unclean. If he touched him, he'd become unclean too, and then he couldn't go into the temple in Jerusalem. He could not risk that.

Besides, maybe it was a trick and the man was only pretending to be injured. There might be others waiting in hiding to ambush anyone who stopped to helped the man. He was no fool; he would not fall for an old trick like that.

The third man: He was just going down the road when he too saw a man on the side of the road and left for dead. It could happen to anyone.

He was a Levite, a man of importance, of education and training. His hands and mind were made for administering the law of Moses for the people. He saw plenty of riffraff in his lifetime. "If you've seen one, you've seen them all," he thought. "And if you help one, word gets around and you are besieged by them all. Better to mind your own business.

Don't make any eye contact. Let people like that take care of their own. A Levite has better things to do than waste his precious time on such as this man. If God wants him to die, may God's will be done." So went the thoughts of the Levite who kept on moving, eyes straight ahead.

The fourth man: He was a scholar, most likely a lawyer, that is, someone steeped in Mosaic Law. He'd come into the town, perhaps to teach future scholars. There was a gathering in town. People crowded around that man some are calling the long-awaited Christ. He mingled in the crowd until he got up close to Jesus. Now was his chance, unexpected, but much appreciated. He'd test this would-be messiah and see if he was really true to the law of Moses. "What a lucky day for me," he thought. "A chance to meet the man from Nazareth, along with his followers. I'll ask him a question to see how he can reply."

"Teacher, what must I do to inherit eternal life?"

Knowing him to be a scholar of the law, Jesus was quick to reply: *"What is written in the law? How do you read it?"*

Clever reply, the scholar thought. "He knows who and what I am. I'll show him up with my knowledge of the Law of Moses." So the scholar quoted Deuteronomy 6:4-5 and Leviticus 19:18: *"You shall love the Lord, your God, with all your heart, with all your being, with all your strength, and with all your mind, and your neighbor as yourself."*

What a bright scholar! He knew the law. And now there seemed to be mutual respect between the scholar and Jesus. So he asked Jesus another question, not to test him as before, but because he wanted to understand who is his neighbor whom he must love so well. This Jesus may be just the insightful man who can answer him.

Four men in the gospel. Each had an accidental meeting. One met robbers, two others met a dying man. Another met Jesus. Four chance meetings. It could happen to anyone.

There was a fifth man. There was the Samaritan. He too had a chance meeting. It could happen to anyone. But it did not happen to anyone. It happened to the Samaritan. And what he did was not by chance. Nor was his love of his neighbor by chance. He did not have to ask anyone who was the neighbor he should love. He did not have to study the law to live the law. He did not need to think of his own welfare to know the need of someone else's welfare.

The sixth person: Now, how about you? What did you tell yourself the last time you passed by your neighbor in need? Was it a beggar, was he old or young, white or black, American or Mexican, sickly or healthy?

If you weren't sure, why did you not ask Jesus if he was your neighbor? Jesus would have told you too. You don't have to be a scholar.

Sister Bridget in Romania

21st Sunday, C: Hebrews 12:5-7, 11-13, Isaiah 66:18-21

If you are looking for an easy way to get to heaven, give it up. There isn't one.

The people who came up to Jesus are concerned about how many people are going to be saved. Jesus' reply calls them, not to focus on how many will be saved, but on themselves, to make sure that, however many there are who enter God's kingdom, they are included in that number.

Good advice for those who heard Jesus, but it was not the end of Jesus' counsel about salvation. The way to salvation, Jesus tells those who seek it, is *through the narrow gate*. Don't look for an easy way to God's kingdom. Seek and strive for the right way, the good way, that is, the way of the Cross, in imitation of Jesus. Entry into the Kingdom of God is not easy, nor is it meant to be.

Jesus calls all who would be his followers to come with him on a journey that is not easy, but has many hardships, challenges and suffering. It is a journey which requires us to share what we have, to forgive those who trespass against us, and to make sacrifices of our time and talents for the good of the others. Jesus did not promise us a paradise in this life, but Paradise in the next life. We are free to build, to tear down, to create or to destroy in this life. History has shown us that there are many who make the earthly journey a difficult challenge.

The narrow gate through which we are called to enter can be pretty narrow for some.

While on my vacation in Romania with two other priests this summer, I learned much about modern-day "narrow gates" through which people entered God's kingdom. I visited the prison camp where hundreds of priests and bishops were incarcerated during the 1950's by a Communist regime which sought to eradicate Catholicism in that country. I walked into the torture room where many were to suffer and die. One of my priest colleagues showed me a photograph on the prison wall. It was a picture of his bishop who was martyred there. My friend cried for his bishop. Then he told me that he began his priestly studies in secret too, but did not have to undergo persecution for his faith and his willingness to follow God's call to priesthood.

The next day I stayed in the guesthouse of a monastery of nuns who taught me more about "narrow gates" and what they mean for those who obey God's call to follow. Most of the nuns were younger, but several made the profession as sisters during the time of the Communist regime (which ended in December 1989). Sister Bridget was the sibling of one of my priest friends. She told us of how they lived as Catholics in the 1980s. Mass was illegal, to be recognized as a priest or sister could mean imprisonment, and for her the process of joining a convent was a real challenge. She had to work a full-time job in one of the Communist factories during the day, then sneak out nights to study with the Mother Superior. Occasional Masses were held during the night only, in private homes, and they moved around the city often so that suspicion would not be aroused by the secret police.

I asked her why she became a nun. She said it was what God called her to do. The circumstances of her country had nothing to do with her desire to know and follow God's will. She did what God wanted her to do. Yes, the gate through which she, and many others, had to travel was narrow. So what?

I asked her if she feared for her life, her safety, her freedom. She said that she never did. They could not take away from her what was in her heart. They could only take away what was around her, not what was inside her. Yes, the gate through which she traveled was narrow. So what?

Sister Bridget is one of the most cheerful and happy people I have ever met. My day at her convent, celebrating Mass, praying, singing, dining together, was perhaps the happiest day I can recall in a long, long time. It was like a taste of heaven on earth. How could those fifteen nuns be so happy, given the difficulties that life has given to them? The answer is perhaps found in the knowledge that they were able to keep their hearts focused on Jesus' call to follow him through a life that promises an eternal life.

The church in Romania is growing, nearly out of control. Since gaining freedom to worship, there are churches being built all over the place, and the seminaries and convents are full to bursting. I don't think anyone there would ever ask Jesus. *"Lord, will only a few people be saved?"* They know the answer:

Jesus' reply calls them, not to focus on how many will be saved, but on themselves, to make sure that, however many there are who enter God's kingdom, they are included in that number.

The way to salvation is *through the narrow gate*. Don't look for an easy way to God's kingdom. Seek and strive for the right way, the good way, the way of the Cross, in imitation of Jesus. Entry into the Kingdom of God is not easy, nor is it meant to be.

You know their story now. It is not a different story for any of ours. As we hear in the reading from the letter to the Hebrews today: *At the time, all discipline seems a cause not for joy but for pain, yet later it brings the peaceful fruit of righteousness to those who are trained by it. So strengthen your drooping hands and your weak knees. Make straight paths for your feet, that what is lame may not be disjointed but healed.*

Ephesus, Pyramids, Native Americans, Twin Towers

23rd Sunday, C: Malachi 3:19-20a, Luke 21:5-19

Jesus said, "All that you see here - the days will come when there will not be left a stone upon another stone that will not be thrown down."

1. I walked with my daughter Elizabeth through the massive white granite ruins of one of the largest of the Roman cities. Located in southeastern Turkey, Ephesus was once a grand city, with a population of over a quarter million. During the height of the Roman Empire, it was located on the crossroads of civilization, on both land and sea routes connecting the East and West of the Empire. St. Paul stayed there, and later wrote his letter to the Ephesian residents to urge them to be strong in their faith. We walked along cobbled streets, and saw the remains of a great library, market places, theaters, and miles and miles of residential homes. It was amazing to see how once such a great city was now this massive ruin, with only faint memories to tell of its greatness. Would the once noble and rich residents of Ephesus ever have believed that their great city would be ruins?

2. The first time I saw the pyramids and rode through the desert of western Egypt, I could not imagine that this desolate and rather impoverished place could ever have been the powerful kingdom that we read about in the Old Testament stories of the Bible. Despite the evidence of the massive pyramids, the intricate carved mausoleums, the literature, and the Bible stories, there was no sign of power and greatness in the present Egypt. Again, I wondered if the great pharaohs and their people would have ever guessed that their centuries of greatness would now be merely the stuff of archeology.

3. A good friend of mine is in the process of donating the family's valuable collection of Native American artifacts and relics to a museum - either the Smithsonian or the state museum. The family has been collecting these artifacts for a long, long time. The places where they were once found are now covered in asphalt, concrete, and modern cities, so that it is no longer possible to obtain these mementos of the Native Americans who once lived abundantly in our nation. They are a peoples whose homes, land, and culture are now reduced to often-romanticized and

adventurous movies and paperbacks. Would they have ever guessed?!

4. Going to work in New York City that morning in early September, 2001, the workers looked up at the massive twin towers soaring above their view, as they entered the building for another day of work. They took for granted the existence of their offices with their furnishings, books, and colleagues. Even if they had been reading the gospel of Luke and saw those words of Jesus: *"All that you see here - the days will come when there will not be left a stone upon another stone that will not be thrown down."* Of course, they would have been wrong. But they could not have known.

Let us look at our gospel of today. Jesus said that the Temple of Jerusalem would be destroyed. Jesus described it clearly in the gospel. And less than forty years after he said those words, it became true as the Roman general Titus led a force into Israel and Jerusalem in A.D. 70, destroying the city, completely decimating the Temple, and killing most of the residents. The survivors fled to the coast, no longer having a temple, a city, a country.

In reality, we know that Jesus was not referring only to Jerusalem and its temple when he said: *"All that you see here - the days will come when there will not be left a stone upon another stone that will not be thrown down."* He was referring to all the created universe, and all within it, and pointing to a time when the world as we know it would end. He was trying to prepare the people, not for visions of doom and gloom, but of hope - hope that a better time and place would be coming, an eternal place of peace and joy, which would replace and supercede the earthly kingdom. As we heard in the first reading from Malachi: *But for you who fear my name, there will arise the sun of justice with its healing rays.* Jesus was telling them, and all of us, that we would all pass away through death in order to rise to new and better life with him.

When you get home, look around you and consider that this too, this home, its furnishings, its treasured mementos will not last forever. That home, with all it has and is, has been given to you to aid you in your journey through life. It is not meant to last forever, nor are we meant to cling to it as if it were all we have and are.

And it is not just our homes and cities which will be passing away. The homes of our bodies will one day pass away too. The body which God gave me to use for my earthly journey is fading - first cataracts which told me the eyes were aging; next was arthritis as I experienced the erosion of the skeletal system; then diverticulitis emerged as the gastrointestinal system started to wear down. Now there is some skin cancer and so too is the skin aging. The temple of our bodies will one day be gone. *Jesus said, "All that you see here - the days will come when there will not be left a stone upon another stone that will not be thrown down."*

If what Jesus said about the Temple of Jerusalem was true also for the mighty empires of Rome and Egypt, of our Native Americans and even our modern buildings, is it so difficult a realization that Jesus' words will be true for each of us? And, if Jesus' words are true, should we not prepare ourselves as if it were going to happen this day?

Angels Led Them to Jesus

Christmas Mass at Midnight: Luke 2:1-14

Do not be afraid, for behold, I proclaim to you good news of great joy ...
Angels appeared to the shepherds and brought them the news that the *Word of God Made Man* had come into their midst. Then they led the shepherds to the place, to see a poor family and meet Jesus the Christ, *an infant wrapped in swaddling clothes, and lying in a manger.*

It was a typical Sunday afternoon last October. I left the church after the Masses and headed for the hospital to visit parishioners. Entering through the emergency room as was my normal routine, I found no one who needed a prayer. So I headed down the corridor of the second floor to the stairway leading down to the first-floor main entrance of the hospital. As I left the reception desk where I got the room numbers I needed, I noticed I was being followed by two boys. They came down the stairs behind me, but I did not pay them any attention at first. Wondering if they were really following me, I headed for the A bank of elevators and pushed the button.

"Are you one of those guys who goes around and prays for people in the hospital?" I heard as I awaited the elevator. I turned around and found two small, very pale identical twin boys. They were two of the most angelic-looking human beings I have ever seek - carrot-colored hair, snow white skin, twinkling eyes, and an open friendliness like one rarely experiences in teenagers. They showed no nervousness or shyness either, but talked to me as if I were their next-door neighbor at home. Before I could say anything, the one on the right repeated his question to me. "Are you one of those guys who goes around and prays for people in the hospital?" I explained that I was a local pastor and came to the hospital often to visit and pray with people. Then, to distract them for a moment so I could think, I asked their ages and which one was the older. The speaker said they were 15 and that he was the older. I was shocked to hear that they were 15 years old; they looked to be 10 or 11. "Would you come and pray with our grandma?" he asked.

I said I had to go upstairs to see someone, but that I would come and meet them later. With no hesitation, they proceeded to board the elevator with me and accompany me to the fourth floor. It was then that I noticed that the younger one was limping very badly. I asked about his limp and he told me about a injury in the yard and woods back home in North Carolina a week ago. He was hard to understand due to his dialect and grammar. Then I tried to tell them they could not go with me to visit patients, but that did not deter them. I stopped the elevator at the third floor, and one was convinced to leave and go to the J wing and wait for me. The other wanted to stay with me to make sure I found his grandma. But when we got to the fourth floor, I made him leave too, with the assurance I would find them on 4th-J shortly.

It was then I realized that these two friendly, trusting, and beautiful boys were very poor and rural twins, that their white skin and very small stature indicated poor nutrition and health, that their trusting natures showed that they had not been in a city much, and that they knew little of social proprieties, or of formal religion either, only that prayer was good, that they did not know how to pray, that I was someone who knew how to pray, and that their grandma needed prayer.

After my visit to our parishioner on 4th A, I debated whether to go to 4th J. After all, I could not just saunter into a patient's room and pray without permission. And I did not even know grandma's name or religion. She might throw me out, and rightly so. But I thought of those trusting boys - those twin red-headed angels were all too compelling to refuse. They seemed to say to me: *Do not be afraid, for behold, I proclaim to you good news of great joy* ...

When I got off the elevator onto the fourth floor of J-wing, the two boys were waiting, with smiles and joy-filled eyes that made me peaceful. "She is in 4413," and they led me around the corner. "What is your grandma's name?" I asked. "She is not our grandma; she's our great-grandma, and her name's Effie."

I took a deep breath, and said my usual prayer: "Here's my heart, here's my hands, here's my mind, and here's my voice, Lord. I give them to you to use." And down the hall we went, into 4413. There were about ten people around a bed, in which a near toothless and hairless woman lay. "We told them you would come," one of the boys announced. They were very simple people, much like the poor shepherds who huddled around Jesus that night when angels called them to a stable. I leaned down, spoke to Effie, then we all took hands and prayed together.

Those two little red-headed angels beamed with joy. Why should they have not? They announced to me the reality of Christ in our midst, and they brought me to a place where Jesus was. And I will never forget that day. Now I know what angels look like. Now I know how it felt for those shepherds in the gospel of Luke on that cold night two thousand years ago. *The angel[s] of the Lord appeared and the glory of the Lord shone about them and they were struck with fear.*

For me, the Christmas event came early this year. In a hospital, in October.

If you have not yet had angels beckoning you to meet the Christ Child, open your hearts anew tonight/today. They are all around you. And not just here, but in your home, your school, your workplace, and they want to show you the Christ Child. Look for them until you find them. *Do not be afraid, for behold, I proclaim to you good news of great joy ...* Don't miss out on Christ this Christmas!

I Never Met a Man Who Had Absolutely Nothing.

6th Sunday, C: Jeremiah 17:5-8

Growing in our selves and in our relationship with God requires freedom - freedom to be who and what we were made by God to be, and to become. As Saint Paul wrote to the Galatians, *For freedom, Christ set us free; so do not submit again to the yoke of slavery.* But freedom can be hard to obtain for most of us. It certainly has been a struggle for me to gain my freedom and overcome my slavery to self.

I suppose I shouldn't have been surprised that nearly everyone who met me as a new priest asked the same two questions. The first question was nearly always: What was it like to give up your home and possessions to become a priest?   My reply was as simple and direct as the question:

Since entering seminary and becoming ordained a priest, I've never known such joy and such peace of mind. When I examine how I have changed, I find that the freedom that I have gained by not being encumbered by so many material possessions is the basis of my peace. When I get up each morning, all I have to think about is whatever God gives me that day to deal with. I don't have to worry about what to wear and what is fashionable; I do not have to fret over a home, its repairs and upkeep, nor be concerned about "keeping up with the Joneses." So what is it like to give up most of the material things I used to have? It is freeing; it removes from me many things on which I depended, but which have no importance in terms of the reason why I live, and die.

The second question I was usually asked was similar: How does it feel being in a lowly position when once you were in positions of stature? And again, my reply was about the same. The more positions of stature one has, the more one has to be concerned with others, what they think, what you need to do for them, and how you can keep your position of status. We have only to look at our elected political leaders to see how having power can make one so focused on pleasing others and not on oneself - certainly not on one's relationship with God and neighbors.   So, in answer to the question about loss of status, my response is like the first one:

As a priest, I have a freedom to focus on today, and not worry about yesterdays or tomorrows. As a priest, I have a freedom to concentrate on others and not on myself. As a priest, I am free to let God use me in whatever way needed, and I do not have to bother with myself. Granted I could have been this way before I was a priest; I do know people who are able to be free from the demands of their positions in life, but they are few. And for me, it was hard to do.

So why am I telling you all this? Because it is what Jesus is telling us in today's gospel. Jesus is teaching the crowds and the disciples about how blessed are the poor, those who are hungry, those who are weeping, and those who are hated. Jesus is telling those who are free from having lots of material goods and free from having power and position that, in their freedom from the things of this earth, they are in a favored position to experience God's love. They are, because of their low positions in this life, more aware of their need for God. They are more able to turn to God to meet their needs, instead of depending on themselves and worldly goods to be their source of security and comfort. The lack of having the things of this earth gives them freedom from those things, and allows them to concentrate on what is really important - being the person they were created to be, a person of which Jeremiah said in our first reading: *Blessed is the one who trusts in the LORD, whose hope is the LORD. He is like a tree planted beside the waters that stretches out its roots to the stream: it fears not the heat when it comes; its leaves stay green; in the year of drought it shows no distress, but still bears fruit.* To such people, Jesus says: *Rejoice and leap for joy on that day! Behold, your reward will be great in heaven.*

But Jesus speaks not just to the lowly in our gospel. He speaks also to the mighty, at least to those who appear mighty in terms of the world's standards. Woe to the rich, woe to those who laugh now, woe to those when all speak well of you. Those who have the security of wealth, happiness with this world, and esteem and respect of others, risk the loss of God because they may be trapped and imprisoned by the things which surround them. The greatest risk of having many possessions is that they may come to possess us. And in that possession of us, we lose our freedom to grow in our relation to ourselves and our God. We can become dependent on others and worldly goods. As Jeremiah warned in our first reading: *Cursed is the one who trusts in human beings, who seeks his strength in flesh, whose heart turns away from the LORD. He is like a barren bush in the desert that enjoys no change of season, but stands in a lava waste, a salt and empty earth.*

So now the point of all this: In his great love for us, Jesus wants us to be free to grow in his love, to become the person we were created to be, so as to one day achieve the goal of our Baptisms - the return to eternity with God. There is nothing essentially wrong with having lots of possessions and high positions. But having much creates strong challenges to overcome. Having much can become a prison, taking away our freedom to be a part of the Body of Christ, a traveler on the journey from baptism to eternal happiness.

Since I have been here at Sacred Heart, I have been incredibly happy and peaceful. It comes from my learning, rather late in life, the message of today's readings about how one achieves freedom from the world's enticements. I have met only one other person that I can say with certainty is more peaceful than I. I will close today by telling you about him. His name is also Charles.

I found Charles in a nursing home one October. He had recently been sent there from a long distance, due to his multiple and chronic debilitating diseases, in order to spend the rest of his life in a bed. In the process of going there, all of Charles' earthly possessions disappeared. When I met him, he had been in that bed for three months, without a visitor, without a friend, without anything. He had no living relative, and no material possession in the world. He wore a hospital gown, and lay on a bed and under a sheet belonging to someone else. I was giving communion to the man beside him when he heard the prayers and called out - not for me, but for the Lord. So I met Charles, the only person I ever have known who had absolutely nothing of this world's goods - no family, no material goods, not even one piece of clothing. And he was so joyful to pray with someone, to receive the Eucharist again after so long. When we arranged to get him some clothes, things for his room, and visitors, he was overjoyed. He could not believe that he could own something again. When I brought him a radio, a crucifix and some clothing, he cried and cried with joy and amazement.

I am certain that Charles was one of the people to whom Jesus was speaking in today's gospel. I am sharing my story today in the hope that I may one day be one of the people to whom Jesus was speaking too. And I am telling you about all this so that you too may be the people to whom Jesus was speaking in today's gospel.

May the words of this holy gospel be in our minds, on our lips, and in our hearts. Amen.

The "Man Who Had Absolutely Nothing" Has Come Home To Us.

Feast of the Holy Family, A: Sirach 3:2-6, 12-14, Matthew 2:13-15, 19-23

"If you live long enough, there won't be any friends to come to your funeral." That is a very true statement. I see it all together too often. Like last weekend when I did a funeral for Paul, an 88-year-old man, whose wife died earlier this year at age 91. There was a beauty to the funeral. Although there were few family members and fewer friends to come to his funeral, there were many parishioners who came. The parishioners did not know the deceased, at least not personally. What they did know was that Paul was a member of this parish and that he was a Catholic who worshiped at this altar for many years. What they did understand was that Paul was their brother, a member of the family of Jesus Christ and, like them, sons and daughters of Christ, hence he was their brother. So they came to the funeral to pray for their brother Paul.

We are all brothers and sisters in Christ. That is why Jesus told us to call God "Our Father," and not "My Father." We are a family, a holy family, and like THE Holy Family whose feast we celebrate this day, we are called to care for each other, to protect and help each other, and, as we saw last week, to mourn and to bury each other. It is what families do. At least, it is what the Family of Christ does.

It is easy, too easy, to forget that we need each other, that we are not Christians in isolation, but Christians in community, and in Communion. If you live to a ripe old age, do you not want your family, your entire parish family, to come and pray for you, and comfort your loved ones, like some did at Paul's funeral last weekend?

A couple of days before Paul's funeral, I was called to visit a local home for adults, to meet a newly arrived man. The director of the home called me and said there was a new resident who said he was Catholic and, although he could not drive, he wanted to come to Mass regularly. When she told me his name, I recognized it and said that he could not be new to the area. I knew Charles, I had anointed him, brought him communion, and prayed with him before. I went to my records and found that Charles was not in my records. That really made me curious because I was just so sure that I knew him. I could close my eyes and see him, and I could describe him. Well, a few days went by and the director of the home called again to ask if we found anyone to give Charles a ride to church on Sundays. I had not yet found anyone, but that name once again rang in my head. I was sure I knew Charles. So I headed for the home, without first calling And I found Charles, looking just as I remembered him. And he was so surprised to see me that he was nearly in tears as he called out his "Hello, Father Charles. Are you in Danville too?"

I had forgotten where and when, but I had met Charles shortly after my ordination to the priesthood when he and I were in a different part of the state. Once, earlier this year, I told you about him in a homily. When I first met him, he was lying under a sheet, with not a single thing to his name - no clothing, no family, no friends, no nothing. In my homily I told you that I had never in my whole life met a person who had absolutely nothing. Back then, my parish adopted Charles and helped him get some clothes, a crucifix and rosary, a radio, some good medical care and, most of all, some friends. That resulted in Charles being transferred away from that home. The parish family into which Charles was adopted was short-lived. But I met him again when I too was transferred. In my next parish assignment, I was sent to a church near Charles again.

I had not seen Charles since then, and that was several years ago. Not until about ten days ago. Now Charles is here in Danville. And we are now his family. We are the only family he has now, and we are likely all the family he will ever have. Although only 61, Charles told me he intends to stay in Danville, and to die here some day. He has a "living will," and with his age and health conditions, he says it is necessary at this time.

In our gospel story for this feast of the Holy Family of Jesus, Mary and Joseph, the focus is on Joseph, and his caring for his family in a difficult time. Herod is killing all the baby boys in the area, and Joseph protects Jesus and his mother. Joseph bundles them up in safety and heads off to Egypt to protect them. The gospel teaches us what it is to be a family - to protect and care for each other, to keep Jesus safe in our midst, and to help all that flee from harm.

Three of our parishioners are now helping Charles get adjusted to Danville, and someone is bringing him to church here. He needs more people to help in getting him to church though. I hope that when you see Charles, you will greet him as your brother in Christ, as a member of a family should. Others have helped him get some clothing once again, and a radio, and a crucifix, and a rosary, and a bible. Some of our parishioners are helping make our parish a Holy Family for someone.

There are many people like Charles in our parish family. Perhaps our family is so large that you don't notice them, or maybe you notice them only once a year when there is an angel tree in the Commons. Our parish family has many brothers and sisters who know no family except us.

Since it is the season for making New Year's resolutions, please, please, make one that you will not ignore your brothers and sisters this year. Please resolve that 2005 will be the year when you, like St. Joseph, will protect the child Jesus in your midst.

Today we praise God for the gift of the Holy Family, for they show us the meaning and purpose of family to all who seek to live as a family here on earth, and who work to become one family in Christ Jesus. We become family, as Jesus, Mary and Joseph show us by their lives, through the daily enactment of faith in each other, hope for each other, and love - a love that is based in working together each day to make our love a visible sign of God's love here and now.

Appendix

Storytelling, Scripture and You

Everyone loves a good story, especially if they are true. Jesus loved a good story too and, in much of his teaching and preaching he was quite a good storyteller. Jesus drew on the experiences around himself. He used those experiences that would be familiar to the people to teach about the Good News of the Kingdom of God. We know many of those endearing stories by heart:

The Good Shepherd
The laborer and the vineyard (Mt. 20:1-16)
Loving one's enemies (Mt 5: 43-48)
Paying taxes (to Caesar) (Mk 12:13-17)
The wheat and the weeds
Parable of the seed (Mk 4:1-29)
Finding a pearl or money
The leaven and the Pharisees (Mt.16: 5-12; Mk 8:14-21)
The danger of riches (Mk 10:17-31)
Mary and Martha (Luke10: 38-42)
Parable of the tenants (Mk 12: 1-12)

And the list goes on and on.

Jesus was a good storyteller, and in his use of settings and contents familiar to his audiences, he brought the Good News to many in ways that were understandable and powerful.

But telling stories requires content. You cannot tell a story, at least not a true one, unless you have some experiences on which to relate to reality, and to the audience. Each of us can be like Jesus in story telling, and this is especially true for older people who have lived a full life, who have experienced much and, through the experiences, have brought the Christian faith and Word of scriptures home into their lived experiences.

Which brings me to the purpose of this presentation - You can be a Story Teller of the Good News of Jesus Christ, just as was Jesus. You have the knowledge of faith, you have heard and read the Scriptures all your life, and you have much "lived" experience on which to relate the

Scriptures. Today I want to challenge you to share your life stories in such a way that they become Gospel Witness.

Many here have complemented me on some of my homilies. I have noticed that the ones most appreciated are the ones in which I draw on life experiences to tell personal stories, in which the message of the scriptures is embedded. What I am doing when I preach in that manner is exactly what I am challenging you to do today. Pray the scriptures by relating them to events and experiences in your life. Even more so, share those stories of your life in which a message of scriptures is taught. You can share by writing, by dictating into a recorder, or by talking. More on that later.

Let me give you an example of how I do it first. Let me take as my scripture the readings of the 16th Sunday in Ordinary Time, Cycle C. The Old Testament is Genesis 18:1-10a and the Gospel is the story of Mary and Martha, found in Luke 10:38-42. I will concentrate on the Gospel principally.

[Read scripture.]
Now the technique is simple, and the steps are obvious:

1. Choose a scripture first. A New Testament piece, especially something from the Synoptic Gospels is a good place to begin. You can also look and choose the day's gospel or the next Sunday gospel.

For me as a priest, this was easy. I chose the next Sunday's readings.

2. Read the scripture prayerfully. Concentrate especially on the characters in the scripture. Reread it, this time imagining that you are one of the characters. Feel what they feel; hear what they hear; react as they might. Do this for each character in the scripture. This may take several readings.

I considered Mary first. Then I recollected on Martha.
I did not reread from Jesus' perspective, but I could have.

3. Now, forget the scripture for the moment, and ask yourself to try to relate something in your life to something you sensed or felt when you were one of the characters in the scripture. Remember there are no good or bad, right or wrong, ways to sense and feel.

- Martha

    She is concerned about good hospitality.

    She would probably have done the same for any guest.

    She was not concentrating on the guest, but on the process of welcoming him.

    Jesus does not really criticize her; he notes that what she does is less important at this moment.

    I'll bet Martha sees her self-worth as based in what she can do.

- Mary

    She is not helping her sister; it seems unfair.

    She overcomes "doing" and chooses to "just be."

    Mary probably sees herself more in terms of being in Christ.

4. Relate some part of your lived experience or an event to something you remember from the scripture you read. What exactly is that word, phrase, section of the scripture which evoked this in you. Go back to the scripture now and note it.

    - I work a lot with elderly, sick, dying. Often they feel worthless, or not important as Christians because they can no longer help others, take care of others, be of service.

    - My own father was feeling depressed and of little worth lately because of the limitations of age and infirmity.

    - Many of us see our self-worth as based in what we do, and not what we are. The phrase which catches me is: "Martha, Martha, you are anxious and upset about so many things."

5. Get ready to make an outline of a story about you or your life or those you know. Making an outline is a good way to do this. Do not worry about style, grammar, etc. Just let your heart and mind lead you to reflect on some part of your life, based on the stimulus of the word or phrase of scripture you chose.

    - Tell about Dad's feeling of worthlessness and where they come from.

    - Tell about how we all define ourselves based on what we can do.

    - Tell how Martha is that way.

    - Tell how Mary is not.

- Explain what Jesus said: "Martha, Martha, ..."
- Relate it back to my father and the others in my life.

6. Now get your story out. Write it down, dictate it into a tape recorder, or tell someone you love, and get them to write or record it.

I choose to write it out by typing.

7. Study and reflect on your story. Re-examine how a moment of your life was a graced moment in which you experienced God's Word. Pray in thanksgiving for this gift. [Read the homily which resulted.]

Now, let me share with you another of my experiences. This time let me share with you how I prepared the homily/story you heard last weekend, the Samaritan Woman at the Well, in John 4:5-41. [Summarize reading, and read homily, making notes aloud.]

The Call to Action: You are and you can be a storyteller of the Good News of Jesus Christ. I implore you to try it just once, setting no expectations on yourself. I assure you that you will find the process a prayerful and grace-filled experience. I am confident you will come to understand why the ordained ministers find preaching and the preparations for preaching such a rewarding and spiritual experience.

The first time you tell your story, using scripture, you may be hesitant to share it with anyone. That is ok. It is sufficient as prayer for yourself.

However, the giftedness of aging is precisely found in the richness of a life of experience in which the vitality of the Good News is made strong. You can be a sharer of the Good News for others. You can share your stories. There are many ways to do it too.

1. Share your stories with your family. Imagine a birthday or holiday gift in which you have inserted a tape or written story of your very own. What a wonderful thing to give something of yourself and your love! Imagine the joy of an adult child or a grandchild hearing or reading a story of you, from a time and place heretofore unknown to them. Imagine, even more so, that in that story of you, there is also a message of faith and love, from scripture.

2. Share the stories with children - at a day care center, in our grade school, etc. so that they may know of the impact of scripture in our lives, so that they may come to experience at a real and human level the message and teachings of Jesus Christ.

3. Share the stories with social clubs, senior centers, or during visits with sick, homebound, and nursing home people. It may stimulate them to do the same. Whatever else, it will give those who can no longer read or write, or even remember, a grace-filled experience of the reality of God's loving presence in each and every human life.

Share your life with others. Share the Good News of Jesus Christ with others. As seniors, you have the experience of living, the grace of many hearings of the scriptures, and you have the gift of time to do it.

SHARING THE TREASURES OF YOUR HEART USING SCRIPTURE

Steps in the process.

1. Choose a scripture first. A New Testament piece, especially something from the Synoptic Gospels is a good place to begin. You can also look and choose the day's gospel or the next Sunday gospel.

2. Read the scripture prayerfully. Concentrate especially on the characters in the scripture. Reread it, this time imagining that you are one of the characters. Feel what they feel; hear what they hear; react as they might. Do this for each character in the scripture. This may take several readings.

3. Now, forget the scripture for the moment, and ask yourself to try to relate something in your life to something you sensed or felt when you were one of the characters in the scripture. Remember there are not good or bad, right or wrong, ways to sense and feel.

4. Relate some part of your lived experience or an event to something you remember from the scripture you read. What exactly is that word, phrase, section of the scripture which evoked this in you. Go back to the scripture now and note it.

5. Get ready to make an outline of a story about you or your life or those you know. Making an outline is a good way to do this. Do not worry about style, grammar, etc. Just let your heart and mind lead you to reflect on some part of your life, based on the stimulus of the word or phrase of scripture you chose.

6. Now get your story out. Write it down, dictate it into a tape recorder, or tell someone you love, and get them to write or record it.

7. Study and reflect on your story. Re-examine how a moment of your life was a graced moment to experience God's Word. Pray in thanksgiving for this gift.

8. Find someone and share it. Like Jesus, tell the Good News of the Kingdom of God.

BIOGRAPHICAL SKETCH: Rev. Charles L. Breindel, Ph.D., is pastor of Sacred Heart Roman Catholic Church, in Danville, Virginia. He was ordained as a priest for the Diocese of Richmond on May 27, 2000. He completed his studies for the priesthood at Catholic University of America, Washington, DC, and lived in seminary formation at Theological College while doing his studies.

A native of St. Marys, Pennsylvania, he was born in 1948. He attended state universities in Pennsylvania, earning a B.S. summa cum laude, M.S., M.A., and Ph.D. prior to his work in health care planning and management.

Prior to entering seminary in 1996, he was director of international development for Virginia Commonwealth University, and Professor of Health Administration, Medical College of Virginia, Richmond Virginia. He has traveled extensively throughout the world, assisting the World Bank, the United States and many other countries in development, particularly in the Middle East and the countries of the former Soviet Union. He has published more than sixty articles, monographs, and book chapters.

He has held executive positions in hospitals, health systems and university. He was also in senior consulting with Arthur Young and Company and Ernst & Young. He has served on many regional, state, and national committees and commissions as well.

On a personal level, he has four grown daughters and has also raised three foster sons. When he can find free time, he enjoys running, mountain hiking, reading, and singing.